A Return to
Common Sense
Reawakening
Liberty
in the
Inhabitants
of
America

Thomas Mullen

Acknowledgments

I wish to express my sincere gratitude to those whose influence has helped inspire this book. First, to my wife and daughter, who remind me daily of why we are here, to Paul Dowling, Ph.D., who introduced me to Locke, to the Wachowski Brothers, who made philosophy cool again, to Dr. Ron Paul, who cured my apathy, to Thomas Zabawa, for teaching me to write, to Thomas Jefferson, one of the four greatest men the world has ever produced, and to John Locke, the father of liberty.

For Abigail, who deserves a chance to be free.

A Return to Common Sense. Reawakening Liberty in the Inhabitants of America

First Published 2009 by:

Thomas Mullen

Apollo Beach, Florida

www.tommullen.net

ISBN 978-1493508792

Book and cover design by Darlene Swanson of Van-garde Imagery, Inc.

Contents

Introduction:
The American Crisis

"THESE are the times that try men's souls. The summer soldier and the sunshine patriot will, in this crisis, shrink from the service of their country; but he that stands it now, deserves the love and thanks of man and woman."

– Thomas Paine (1776)[1]

America finds itself in a time of crisis. For several generations we have expressed dissatisfaction with government, whether with the Viet Nam war, the energy and economic crises of the 1970's, the scandals of the 1980's and 1990's, or the present wars in the Middle East. While a little dissatisfaction with the status quo is healthy, it has gone far beyond that now. For anyone remotely in touch with the state of our republic, there is a growing sense of dread that whatever is wrong is getting much worse much faster. They realize that what was once a desire for change has now become a dire need for change. Yet, in as much as the voting public clamors for it, does anyone think for a moment that the majority of people in America actually know what changes are necessary, or even what changes they want?

The United States emerged from the 19th century during the most innovative period in the history of mankind. The industrial revolution had wrought miracles that could barely have been imagined 100 years before. After thousands of years of traveling on foot or on the backs of beasts of burden, automobiles carried Americans wherever they wished to go. Steamships freed travel by sea from the vagaries of the four winds, and the telegraph and telephone made communication with distant locations instantaneous, when just a few decades earlier weeks or even months might be required for a single letter to arrive. Electric light replaced gas lamps, and man's most ancient dream was realized by Wilbur and Orville Wright.

With the explosion of technology came an explosion of wealth and prosperity. Mass production and other improvements made manufactured goods cheaper, increasing their availability beyond the affluent to the common man. Indeed, as significant as the fortunes that were made by famous captains of industry was rising living standards of the growing middle class and even of the poor. For the first time in history, the common people were the prime market for the output of society's production. After thousands of years, children no longer had to toil with their parents just to ensure that the family had enough to eat. The average American lived comfortably on the income produced by one member of the family and that family's standard of living was constantly improving. No challenge seemed too formidable for a people that had harnessed the power of lightning, conquered the air and seemingly made a servant of Mother Nature herself. Finally, the end of poverty and want were in sight.

At the dawn of the 21st century, no such optimism prevailed. The technology-fueled prosperity of the 1990's had hit a serious stumbling block with the crash of the NASDAQ index. A recession was just getting underway when America welcomed a new president. In the midst of economic doldrums, socio-political disaster occurred. Commercial airplanes exploded into the World Trade Center as a nation and world looked on in horror. The buildings fell down and the War on Terror began.

Over a decade later, the United States finds itself quagmired in that war beyond anyone's expectations. Despite the fact that the Democrats won the

White House and the House has changed hands twice since 9/11, there is still no end in sight to the wars in the Middle East. President Obama began his campaign as an anti-war candidate, but has made it clear that he will continue the U.S. government's policy of military intervention in the Middle East. As the budget deficits and loss of lives mount, Americans are left to wonder if we will be at war forever.

At home, we find ourselves in economic crisis. The stock market has experienced another historic crash, and for the second time in the past century we are told that we face a Great Depression. While 50 years ago, the average American family was comfortably supported by one income, both parents in that family typically work today, and a second job for at least one parent is not uncommon. While doctor bills were once only a concern for those with unusual medical needs, the typical American family is more and more being forced to choose between healthcare and other basic necessities. While past generations saved for a comfortable retirement, the average American today is deep in debt.

How could a century that started with such promise end with so much doubt? Where did we go wrong? Since her historic founding, America has been known as the "land of the free." Yet, the answers proposed for each of our problems involves Americans giving up some of that freedom. However, if freedom is what made America great, why would less freedom make things better now?

We are told "the world changed on September 11, 2001." Is this true? Is the world fundamentally different than it was? Do evil people really hate us enough because of our freedom and prosperity to commit heinous acts of murder against us? Or are there other reasons? Do we really have to surrender some of our freedom in exchange for security against this new threat? What if the threat continues to increase?

Similarly, we are told our economic crisis was caused by too much laissez faire capitalism and too little regulation. Can too much economic freedom really harm us? Will the massive new government programs and "reregulation" promised by our new President solve our problems? What if they don't? Will even less freedom be the answer then?

This book will set out to answer those questions. In order to do so, we must take a sober look in the mirror. In order to know what has put America in decline, it is necessary first to understand what made her great. At a time when most people are confused and searching for answers, we must shine the light of clarity on every aspect of our society. At times, that light may reveal truths we are not ready to face, including the part each of us has played in bringing about our nation's decline.

We must question institutions we have long ago come to think of as unquestionable. The past 100 years in America has been a time of significant change. Of course, the 20th century was a time of astounding technological advancement. However, we have also made ideological changes that have made America into a much different kind of society than the one our founders built. Were those changes improvements, or have we moved away from the principles that made us great? Are we still the "land of the free?" Are we still the "land of opportunity? Do we really know what those cherished words mean?

During the past few decades of apparent prosperity, very few of us wished to be bothered with the endless partisan bickering of our politicians, despite our frequent expressions of dissatisfaction with them. While we may not have agreed with much about the direction in which our leadership was taking our country, we did not connect what was happening in Washington, D.C. with our own lives or the lives of our families. We have been in a kind of slumber, believing that a free and open society of opportunity and prosperity is guaranteed in America, regardless of the decisions of politicians that determine what kind of society we are.

One thing is certain. We are out of time. In past decades, we have talked about issues we feared may present significant problems for the America of the future. That future is here. It is no longer enough to wistfully talk about the America we will leave to our children. Everything we hold dear about America is in jeopardy, and the time has come to act

Chapter 1
What is Freedom?

"And what is this liberty, whose very name makes the heart beat faster and shakes the world?"

– Frederic Bastiat[1] (1850)

If there is one thing uniquely associated with America, it is freedom. From the moment Cornwallis surrendered to Washington at Yorktown, America has been a symbol of liberty to the entire world. Since the end of World War II, when the United States assumed a worldwide leadership role, it has been the leader of the "free world." At sporting events, standing crowds begin their ovation when the vocalist singing the national anthem gets to the words, "O'er the land of the free." Even in everyday conversations, scarcely a day goes by that one does not hear someone say, "Do what you like, it's a free country."

Although we all agree that America is the "land of the free," there are questions about freedom that might be more difficult to answer. What is freedom? How is it defined? What makes America the land of the free? How would we know if we were to lose our freedom? What is it that our soldiers die for and our politicians swear to defend?

We have been told a lot of things about what freedom is not. From the end of World War II until 1991, most Americans understood that freedom was not communism. For almost three generations, Americans lived in the "free world" during its cold war with the communist Eastern Bloc. Without further thought or instruction, many children of the 20th century think of freedom merely as the antithesis of communism. In some ways, this is not completely untrue, although it hardly provides a complete answer to our question.

Certainly, the mere absence of communism doesn't necessarily guarantee freedom. The 18th century British monarchy wasn't communist, but the American colonists nevertheless considered it tyrannical enough to rebel against. Likewise, the Royal House of Saud may be an ally of the U.S. government, but most Americans would not regard Saudi Arabia as a "free country."

In addition to monarchies, there are plenty of dictatorships around the world that don't enforce a communist system but are nevertheless oppressive. While they also may be allies of the U.S. government, they certainly aren't free countries, either. So, a society is not free merely because it is not communist.

On the other hand, monarchy doesn't seem to necessarily preclude freedom, either. Great Britain has been a relatively free country throughout much of its history, even when the monarchy was much more than a figurehead. The American Revolution notwithstanding, Great Britain was at that time one of the freest societies in the world. Therefore, rather than conclude that no freedom is possible under a monarchy, one might instead conclude that monarchies neither guarantee nor necessarily exclude freedom. Freedom or tyranny seems possible under almost any system of government.

Perhaps we can define freedom more easily by looking at its antithesis. Merriam-Webster Dictionary lists slavery among antonyms for freedom. Surely, we have found a start here. Most people would agree that slavery is the complete absence of freedom. Who can we imagine that is less free than the slave? This is helpful in beginning to try to frame an answer, but freedom cannot be merely the absence of slavery. Surely our founding fathers bled to give us a higher standard than this!

If we are told anything about what freedom is, it is that freedom is democracy. If you ask most Americans, this is the answer you will get. This is reinforced ad nauseum by politicians, media, and teachers in our public schools. When Iraq held its first elections after the overthrow of Saddam Hussein, politicians and journalists universally celebrated the Iraqis' "first taste of freedom."

Certainly, democracy is a vast improvement over the autocratic rule of a dictator. But does democracy automatically mean freedom? If democracy is rule by the majority, what about the minority? What if 51 % of the people voted to oppress the other 49%? Would that society truly be free?

Most Americans would be quite surprised to learn what our founding fathers thought about democracy. Any objective analysis would conclude that their feelings lay somewhere between suspicion and contempt.

James Madison said, "Democracy is the most vile form of government ... democracies have ever been spectacles of turbulence and contention: have ever been found incompatible with personal security or the rights of property: and have in general been as short in their lives as they have been violent in their deaths,"[2]

In a letter to James Monroe, he also said,

"There is no maxim, in my opinion, which is more liable to be misapplied, and which, therefore, more needs elucidation, than the current one, that the interest of the majority is the political standard of right and wrong."[3]

While often extolling the virtue of majority rule, Thomas Jefferson nevertheless wrote,

"...that the majority, oppressing an individual, is guilty of a crime, abuses its strength, and by acting on the law of the strongest breaks up the foundations of society."[4]

Can this be true? The founding fathers were ambivalent about democracy? For many people, this is tantamount to sacrilege. More shocking still is what the Declaration of Independence and the U.S. Constitution say about democracy: nothing. Nowhere in our founding documents will you find the word "democracy" or the assertion, implicit or explicit, that our government is a democracy. How can this be?

Despite what we are taught virtually from birth, the United States of America has never been a democracy. As only contrarians point out these days, it is a constitutional republic. We choose our leaders using the democratic process of majority vote, but that is the extent to which the United States involves itself with democracy.

Like monarchy, democracy neither guarantees nor necessarily prohibits freedom. Our founders actually feared that democracy poses a danger to freedom. Apart from the pure heresy of the idea, it leaves us with a problem. We are no closer to defining freedom. If even democracy is not freedom, perhaps freedom doesn't really exist! If we are not to find freedom in democracy, where else can we look?

We certainly won't learn what freedom is from our politicians. While terrorism, healthcare, unemployment, gay marriage, and a host of other "major issues" dominate public debate, freedom is just too quaint, too academic, or too forgotten to get any airplay. Yet, as we shall see as we explore the different subjects of this book, freedom is the fundamental issue. In fact, despite what we perceive as a myriad of different problems facing the United States of America today, freedom is actually the *only issue*. That may be hard to accept, given the decades of shoddy history, obfuscation, and plain old bad ideas we've been bombarded with. Nevertheless, our greatest challenges and their solutions revolve around freedom. If freedom is really that important, we'd better be absolutely sure we know what it is.

In order to answer the question posed by Bastiat at the beginning of this chapter, we will have to go back to the beginning. Our founding fathers faced no such quandary about the definition of freedom. They knew exactly what it was. They were children of the Enlightenment, and derived their ideas about freedom directly from its philosophers, especially John Locke. While these philosophers were powerful thinkers and their ideas were (no pun intended) revolutionary at the time, the principles of liberty are relatively simple. They are, as the namesake of this book concluded, common sense. It was an understanding of these revolutionary ideas by average American colonists that inspired the revolution that gave birth to a nation.

The idea that opens the door to the true meaning of freedom is individual rights. Despite the emphasis today on the "general welfare" and the "common good," the American tradition of liberty has nothing to do with either. Instead, the founders believed each individual was born with natural, inalienable rights. The Declaration of Independence states,

"We hold these truths to be self evident, that all men are created equal, that they are endowed by their Creator with certain unalienable Rights," [5]

This passage is quoted widely in popular culture. Invariably, the words emphasized are "that all men are created equal." Certainly, these are fine words and worthy of veneration. However, the rest of this passage is equally important. Every human being, *because* of his equality with all other human beings, has rights no earthly power can take away. These rights are "unalienable," so that governments, even democratically elected governments, have no power to revoke them. To the founding fathers this was self-evident. It was true based purely upon man's existence itself.

This idea is drawn directly from the philosophy of John Locke, who wrote,

"A state also of equality, wherein all the power and jurisdiction is reciprocal, no one having more than another; there being nothing more evident, than that creatures of the same species and rank, promiscuously born to all the same advantages of nature, and the use of the same faculties, should also be equal one amongst another without subordination or subjection," [6]

While these rights are endowed by a Creator, the founders did not specify who the Creator was. Too often, those arguing for the ideals of our republic make the fatal mistake of basing the natural rights upon belief not only in God, but specifically upon the Christian God. While the founders were by no means opposed to Christianity, belief in it or even in God is not a prerequisite for the existence of the natural rights. The beauty of this idea is that it transcends religion and thus welcomes members of all religions, and those with no religious beliefs at all. Therefore, the first building block of freedom, individual, inalienable rights, can be claimed by Christians, Muslims, Jews, Buddhists, Hindus, atheists, by every person on earth.

So what are these inalienable rights, which cannot be taken away? The Declaration goes on to say, "That among these are Life, Liberty, and the Pursuit of Happiness."[7]

At first glance, this statement might be a bit deceiving, maybe even a little disappointing. Life, Liberty, and the Pursuit of Happiness? Is that all? Surely we have more rights than these! Of course, the Declaration says "among these," so it does not limit the natural rights to these three. But these three are important. It is worthwhile to determine the meaning of each.

The right to life is pretty easy to understand. Most civilized societies have laws against murder. Each individual has a right not to be killed by another human being, except in self-defense. So far, so good. What about the other two? We are in the midst of trying to define liberty, or freedom, so let us put that aside for the moment. The third right listed is "the pursuit of happiness." What does that mean? Does it mean nothing? Or does it mean everything? What if it makes me happy to steal cars or blow up buildings? Surely, I don't have a right to pursue happiness like that!

No. There is a natural limit on liberty and the pursuit of happiness. Again, we can find the answer in Locke,

"To understand political power right, and derive it from its original, we must consider, what state all men are naturally in, and that is, a state of perfect freedom to order their actions, and dispose of their possessions and persons, as they think fit, within the bounds of the law of nature, without asking leave, or depending upon the will of any other man." [8]

While people are free to do what they want, they must do so "within the bounds of the law of nature." What is the law of nature? Locke goes on to tell us,

"The state of nature has a law of nature to govern it, which obliges every one: and Reason, which is that law, teaches all mankind, who will but consult it, that being all equal and independent, no one ought to harm another in his life, health, liberty, or possessions..." [9]

Finally, we have some indication of what freedom is, rather than what it is not. Liberty is not the unlimited ability to do whatever you want, nor is it confined to the arbitrary limits placed upon people by governments. Contrary to the spurious argument that unfettered liberty would result in chaos, we see that the law of nature, Reason, very clearly and unambiguously prohibits some actions, even for people in a state of absolute liberty. They are:

1. Initiating the use of force or violence

2. Infringing upon another person's liberty

3. Harming them in their possessions.

This last limit upon the actions of free individuals is important. Locke spends an entire chapter of his Second Treatise talking about it. It is related to property, which is arguably the most important right, while at the same time the least understood. Property is important enough that we will spend the next chapter examining the subject. To do this we will have to come to a clear definition of property, including how it is acquired, how it is exchanged, and what right the owner has to it.

More importantly, we have arrived at a definition of liberty. It is the right of any person to do as they please, as long as they do not violate the equal rights of anyone else. The latter half of this definition is generally referred to as the "non-aggression principle." Political activists associate this principle with libertarians, while intellectuals associate it with Ayn Rand's philosophy of Objectivism. Certainly both movements recognize and venerate it, but it is important to realize that neither is its source. In fact, the non-aggression principle has been articulated with very little variation by all writers in the liberal tradition, including Locke, Jefferson, Paine, Bastiat, Mill, and later Rand and other 20th century writers and thinkers.

By applying this principle, the most complicated societal issues become astoundingly simple. The ambiguous becomes unambiguous. The answers become clear. Virtually every problem facing America today can be solved by applying the principle of freedom.

There are a few points we should review for emphasis. First, the rights mentioned in the Declaration of Independence and drawn out of Locke's philosophy are inalienable. They cannot be taken away by any power on earth, including a majority vote. The reason the founders were suspicious of democracy was because of their fear that the majority would oppress the individual by voting away the individual's rights, especially property rights. This was the reason for the separation of powers and the limits on government authority. Even a majority vote can be a threat to freedom.

The difference between a right and a privilege is a vital concept to understand. A right is something you are born with, that you possess merely because you exist. A privilege is something that is granted by another person, group, or a government. Our country was founded upon the principle that all people have inalienable rights that cannot be taken away, not privileges granted by their government. As John Adams so eloquently put it,

"I say RIGHTS, for such they have, undoubtedly, antecedent to all earthly government, — Rights, that cannot be repealed or restrained by human laws — Rights, derived from the great Legislator of the universe."[10]

There is no need to be "thankful for the rights we have in America." All people have those rights and gratitude is neither necessary nor appropriate. Rather, people are justified in demanding their rights, and any violation of them should be recognized as an act of aggression.

Second, in any conflict between individual liberty and the will of the majority, individual liberty prevails without compromise. The majority has no right to violate the rights of the individual. This is to some extent merely making the first point in reverse, but it is important enough to say in more than one way. Society doesn't have rights; individuals do. Society is nothing more than a collection of individuals, so protecting each individual in society protects society.

Despite these seemingly undeniable truths, individual liberty is today under constant attack because of its perceived conflict with the common good or "the needs of society." While living together and agreeing not to initiate aggression against each other seems astoundingly simple, our politicians would have us believe there is something incredibly complicated about it. They create a world in which civil society is a maze of moral dilemmas that only their astute guidance can lead us safely through. Once liberty is properly understood and applied, all of these supposed dilemmas disappear.

Chapter 2
Property Rights

"Among the natural rights of the Colonists are these: First, a right to life; Secondly, to liberty; Thirdly, to property; together with the right to support and defend them in the best manner they can. These are evident branches of, rather than deductions from, the duty of self-preservation, commonly called the first law of nature."

– Samuel Adams (1772)[1]

Most 21st century Americans have very little understanding of property rights. To most people, the word property itself first conjures up the image of real estate, although most people would also recognize their "stuff" as property. However, the vital component of property is not your house, your new stereo system, or the money in your bank account. While most Americans would not stand for this type of property being seized without their consent, they stand by passively while their most precious property is forcibly taken from them: their labor.

All property has its origins in labor. The only way for wealth to be created is for man to mix his effort, or labor, with natural resources. By mixing his labor with nature, man creates property. His ownership of it is derived from the labor he invested into it. This is not only an inalienable right; it is the central right. Man's survival depends upon it. While a human being can survive indefinitely without the freedoms of speech, religion, or the press, however unjust those conditions might be, he cannot survive more than a few days without food and water. Even a man stranded alone on an island must work to pick fruit from the trees, or hunt animals for the meat he needs to survive. He must work to produce the means of his survival and the fruits of his labor are his alone to dispose of as he wishes. Locke speaks directly to this most important of rights.

"He that is nourished by the acorns he picked up under an oak, or the apples he gathered from the trees in the wood, has certainly appropriated them to himself. Nobody can deny but the nourishment is his. I ask then, when did they begin to be his? when he digested? or when he eat? or when he boiled? or when he brought them home? or when he picked them up? and it is plain, if the first gathering made them not his, nothing else could. That labour put a distinction between them and common: that added something to them more than nature, the common mother of all, had done; and so they became his private right. And will any one say, he had no right to those acorns or apples, he thus appropriated, because he had not the consent of all mankind to make them his? Was it a robbery thus to assume to himself what belonged to all in common? If such a consent as that was necessary, man had starved, notwithstanding the plenty God had given him. We see in commons, which remain so by compact, that it is the taking any part of what is common, and removing it out of the state nature leaves it in, which begins the property; without which the common is of no use. And the taking of this or that part does not depend on the express consent of all the commoners. Thus the grass my horse has bit; the turfs my servant has cut; and the ore I have digged in any place, where I have a right to them in common with others, become my property, without the assignation or consent of any body. The labour that was mine, removing them out of that common state they were in, hath fixed my property in them."[2]

One could write volumes about this one paragraph alone, but the essential idea is that property has its roots in labor. Once labor has been mixed with natural resources held in common, the resulting product becomes the property of the laborer. The concept of "commons" is important to understand. Locke does not justify going onto private property and picking fruit from someone else's trees. Once land has been purchased, the fruit is no longer held in common. It is the property of the landowner and cannot be taken without the landowner's consent.

Once property has been created, it can then be exchanged. The essence of a free society is the ability of its citizens to exchange property voluntarily. In order to acquire property one has not created oneself, one must obtain the consent of its current owner. This is usually done in a trade, where each party offers the other property he deems of equal value to the property he desires. If both parties are willing to trade, the sale is made.

The crucial element of free trade is not fair compensation, but mutual, voluntary consent. Like all other human interaction, the exchange of property is subject to the non-aggression principle. Anyone is free to give away his property without being compensated. If he has done so voluntarily, then the recipient has acquired the property legitimately, even though he offered no compensation in return. Conversely, property cannot be acquired legitimately *without* the consent of its owner even if compensation is made. If someone were to forcibly take your car at gunpoint, he would not have acquired it legitimately even if he left you with money equaling ten times the car's worth. Without mutual, voluntary consent, there is no legitimate exchange of property.

The majority of people today do not acquire their property by mixing their labor directly with nature, but by mixing it with someone else's property, usually in an employer/employee relationship. When an employment contract is made, the employee goes to the workspace the employer has provided and uses materials and resources owned by the employer to produce some good or service. That good or service is the property of the employer to sell or consume as the employer sees fit. The employee owned his labor, which he agreed to sell to the employer for a mutually agreed price: his wages. While the employer owns the product the employee produced, the wages earned are the employee's compensation for his labor and are his property.

As wealth is created or acquired, it is also consumed. When an apple grower trades his apples for another's oranges, each walks away and eats the newly acquired fruit, along with some portion of his own fruit. What is not eaten immediately can be saved for another day. While the apple grower can only save his surplus apples until they spoil, money allows him to sell all of his surplus apples to others, but still save their value in accumulated money. We will deal with the important concept of money in a later chapter, but for now it is sufficient to recognize it as a store of value. It is accepted in exchange for goods and services, and becomes the recipient's property.

Using money, a person is able to store up the difference between what he has produced and what he has consumed indefinitely. This is generally referred to as "savings." Savings have a variety of uses. The most commonly recognized use is to sustain consumption during times when one is producing less than one consumes, or producing nothing at all, such as during retirement. In a vibrant, productive economy, it is possible for a person to cease producing wealth via his labor and live the remaining years of his life on his savings, the result of decades of producing more than he consumes.

Savings play another role in society. Savings also become capital, the means of production. In order to produce anything beyond the goods that can be acquired directly from nature, capital goods are necessary, such as machines, factories, farming equipment, or other means of production. Almost no new business can be started without savings, or capital, because there would be no way to put the productive structure in place, including paying the employees whose labor is necessary in order to produce the first goods or services. The person who supplies this needed capital is a "capitalist," and the recognition that the proceeds from that investment of capital are the capitalist's property is "capitalism." We will explore the relationship between capitalism and liberty in a later chapter.

As control over the fruits of one's labor are necessary to sustain one's existence, it is clear that property rights are among the most basic, most important rights. If people have a right to life, they must have property rights or they cannot sustain their lives or pursue their happiness. As Samuel Adams put it, property is an evident branch of self-preservation.

Once the connection between property and labor is understood, the interdependence of life, liberty, and property is undeniable. All consumption must be preceded by production and production can only occur through human labor. In fact, there is no way for an individual to pursue any goal, whether material, intellectual, or spiritual, without labor. Even the search for God requires an intellectual and spiritual effort. It cannot commence without labor.

To truly understand the importance of property rights, one must consider a further aspect of labor. It is not just the exertion of mind and body necessary to produce some good or service. That exertion happens over time, the hours or days of our lives; hours and days which cannot be replaced once they are spent.

Therefore, when human beings trade their goods or services with one another, they are really trading pieces of their lives. If they have exchanged their labor for money, that money now contains some part of their lives, a part that can never be reclaimed. That is why the same verb is used for both money and time. Both are "spent" in exchange for some benefit.

One cannot be free if one does not own his labor and the product of his labor.

To deny a human being ownership of his labor is to deny his right to life itself, for he now lives only at the arbitrary whim of whoever has control of his labor. For such a person, life is a privilege granted by someone else, rather than a right.

Consider the condition of man in the complete absence of property rights. This is the proper definition of slavery. Perhaps because property rights have faded so far from popular consciousness, our concept of slavery has become blurred in recent decades. Today, most people seem to associate slavery primarily with captivity, chains, abuse, and poor living conditions. Certainly all of these horrors accompanied slavery, but they are not the essence of slavery.

Slave owners had no fascination with holding captives, nor were they for the most part sadistic monsters who abused people for their own amusement. No, what the slave owner wanted was not a captive, but the free labor he could extract without the slave's consent. This is why freedom and slavery are opposites. Freedom recognizes property rights. Slavery does not.

Slavery also helps clarify why voluntary consent, not compensation, is the fundamental basis of property rights. We don't consider volunteers at a charity event slaves, even though they are not compensated for their labor. That's because they have voluntarily offered their labor to the organizers. Conversely, we don't call slaves "volunteers," however much that euphemism might ease the conscience of the slaveholder! That's because the slave has not voluntarily offered his services to the slave owner. The most meaningful definition of slavery is using coercion to obtain a person's labor without his consent.

In economic terms, we have two identifiable extremes. Freedom is defined by recognition of each individual's right to the fruits of his labor. Slavery is the denial of this right. More than anything else, it is where a society falls between these two extremes that determines whether or not it is free. The

United States was once as close to the freedom extreme as possible. Today, that is far from true.

In summary, life, liberty, and property are the essential rights. Man's survival depends upon them. While most political groups in America at least rhetorically claim to support life and liberty, the same cannot be said in regards to the inalienable right to the fruits of one's labor. Yet, it is recognition of this right, above all others, that makes us free. It is denial of this right, above all others, that makes us slaves.

Chapter 3
The Role of Government

"Our legislators are not sufficiently apprised of the rightful limits of their powers; that their true office is to declare and enforce only our natural rights and duties, and to take none of them from us. No man has a natural right to commit aggression on the equal rights of another; and this is all from which the laws ought to restrain him."

– Thomas Jefferson (1816)[1]

It is no wonder so small a percentage of the population votes in U.S. elections. Today, politics is made to seem so complicated that one would have to quit his job and study it full time to get even a superficial understanding of the issues. We are given the impression that a range of issues constitute moral dilemmas where competing but equally worthy interests must be considered and an equitable compromise reached. How do we enact legislation that supports labor while not constricting economic growth? How do we fight hate crimes while preserving free speech? How do we support Israel without inflaming further hatred among Muslims? How will we ensure that every American has access to affordable healthcare?

Presidential elections present us with more impossible choices. One candidate seems better qualified to manage the economy and has a better energy policy. The other seems more prepared to lead U.S. efforts overseas in foreign policy and promoting democracy. We may like one's policy on gay marriage or abortion, while preferring another's on freedom of religion. Must we always feel like we are choosing the lesser of two evils?

None of these dilemmas are real. A government performing the tasks delegated to it in the U.S. Constitution faces no such conflicts. It needn't answer any of the questions posed above, nor require any of those positions from its presidential candidates. As surprising as it may seem, our government was never intended to manage the economy, provide healthcare, prevent crime, enact energy policy, promote democracy abroad, or fight unemployment. When the government attempts to do these things, it is not merely "overachieving," but is actually acting counter to its purpose. To most Americans of the 21st century, these statements might seem shocking. If government is not supposed to be doing any of these things, then what is it supposed to be doing?

Locke had this to say about the purpose of government,

"The great and chief end, therefore, of men's uniting into commonwealths, and putting themselves under government, is the preservation of their property."[2]

Was Locke oversimplifying? Surely the role of government can't be as simple as that!

Locke was able to make that remarkable statement by preceding it with this one,

"This makes him willing to quit a condition, which, however free, is full of fears and continual dangers: and it is not without reason, that he seeks out, and is willing to join in society with others, who are already united, or have a mind to unite, for the mutual preservation of their lives, liberties and estates, which I call by the general name, property."[3]

According to Locke, the purpose of government is the protection of our lives, liberty, and property. That is certainly something quite different than what we've been told. Is this merely the views of one philosopher in the liberal tradition? Perhaps the founders admired Locke but here departed from his opinions. Let us consult them directly. The Declaration of Independence speaks directly to the purpose of government,

"...that they are endowed by their Creator with certain inalienable Rights, that among these are Life, Liberty and the pursuit of Happiness. That to secure these rights, Governments are instituted among Men, deriving their just powers from the consent of the governed,"[4]

We examined the natural, inalienable rights in the first chapter. We see here that the purpose of government is to secure those rights. The document does not say, "to secure these rights, to manage the economy, to fight unemployment, to ensure universal healthcare...." The sole purpose of government is to protect the rights of each individual.

However, must government be limited to this purpose, or can government provide its citizens with more? Locke tells us that,

"A man, as has been proved, cannot subject himself to the arbitrary power of another; and having in the state of nature no arbitrary power over the life, liberty, or possession of another, but only so much as the law of nature gave him for the preservation of himself, and the rest of mankind; this is all he doth, or can give up to the common-wealth, and by it to the legislative power, so that the legislative can have no more than this."[6]

He goes on to say,

"Thirdly, The supreme power cannot take from any man any part of his property without his own consent: for the preservation of property being the end of government, and that for which men enter into society, it necessarily supposes and requires, that the people should have property, without which they must be supposed to lose that, by entering into society, which was the end for which they entered into it; too gross an absurdity for any man to own.

Men therefore in society having property, they have such a right to the goods, which by the law of the community are theirs, that nobody hath a right to take their substance or any part of it from them, without their own consent: without this they have no property at all; for I have truly no property in that, which another can by right take from me, when he pleases, against my consent. Hence it is a mistake to think, that the supreme or legislative power of any commonwealth, can do what it will, and dispose of the estates of the subject arbitrarily, or take any part of them at pleasure."[7]

In The Rights of Man, Thomas Paine writes,

"Every man wishes to pursue his occupation, and to enjoy the fruits of his labours and the produce of his property in peace and safety, and with the least possible expense. When these things are accomplished, all the objects for which government ought to be established are answered."[8]

To the philosophers in the liberal tradition, the answer is clear. Government power can go no farther than protecting the life, liberty, and property of its constituents. Government is merely the societal extension of the individual right of self-defense. As society is no more than a collection of individuals, those individuals cannot delegate a power to government that they do not possess individually. As Jefferson so eloquently expressed in the prologue to this chapter, government is allowed only to protect us from aggression against our rights. It has no other purpose and is allowed no other power. Put most succinctly, government's role is to enforce the non-aggression principle. When government attempts to do more, it is initiating aggression itself and contradicting the very reason for its existence.

This statement requires some explanation. In a society where government is no longer viewed as a protector of rights, but as a "provider of services," it is easy to forget what the nature of government action is. All government action, whether law enforcement, military action, economic policy, or even providing medical care is carried out by force. This is the elephant hiding in the corner of modern political discussion. We pretend government action is something other than coercion, but it isn't. We have become so desensitized to coercion that many people seem to forget that there is nothing "voluntary" about anything government does.

When government passes a law or levies a tax, that law or tax is backed by the threat of violence. If you violate the law or refuse to pay the tax, you are subject to prosecution. If you fail to appear to answer the charges, you will be arrested. If you resist the arrest, you will be forcefully subdued. If you resist further, you will be killed. This is the true nature of government. There is no choice involved. Government is nothing more than the collective use of force. This is the reason the founders believed government should be so severely limited. As George Washington put it,

"Government is not reason, it is not eloquence; it is force; like fire, a troublesome servant and a fearful master. Never for a moment should it be left to irresponsible action."[9]

We have forgotten these principles entirely and with them has gone our liberty. While we recognize that individuals are only allowed to use force in self-defense, we have become addicted to appealing to government, the collective use of force, to address every issue in society that displeases us. Whenever we do so we allow government to violate the very rights it exists to protect. Each time, we surrender a little more of our freedom.

It is easy to lose sight of this when government begins to perform functions far removed from its core purpose. For example, our federal government hundreds of billions per year providing medical services to the poor and elderly. Our perception of these programs (Medicare and Medicaid) is that they are "services" that are paid for "by government." However, government doesn't have any of its own money. Every dollar paid out by the government must be taken from somebody else. The "contributors" to these programs don't fund them by consent. As the old saying tells us, taxpayers have no more choice about paying taxes than they do about dying.

In plain English, Medicare is government forcing individuals to pay for healthcare services for other people, under the threat of violence if they refuse. It is a clear violation of the non-aggression principle. Stripped of euphemism and spin, the same is true for every government social program. Seen for what they truly are, it might be more appropriate to call them "anti-social programs."

This same reasoning applies to Social Security, welfare, Medicaid, food stamps, HEAP, corporate subsidies, farm subsidies, corporate bailouts and much more. Our government forcibly redistributes wealth for the rich, the poor, and everyone in between. When there is debate regarding these programs, it always revolves around how best to pay for them or how they should be "reformed." There is never a discussion questioning whether these programs should exist at all. All debate assumes these programs must exist, but never where the government gets the authority to run them.

In addition to the clear moral repugnancy of the programs, they are also ineffective. As we will see in a later chapter, government's violation of property rights is the root cause of most of the economic problems that America faces today. Over and over when looking at what we are told are complicated issues, we will find that applying the non-aggression principle makes them astoundingly simple.

Despite politicians' rhetoric about the "new challenges of the 21st century," these concepts were well-known to our founding fathers. While socialism was not a dominant political philosophy yet, the founders were certainly familiar with the concept of government wealth redistribution and were unambiguously against it. It is ironic that the Democrats, traditional champions of these programs, claim to be the party of Jefferson, while on this one issue alone Jefferson would disown them completely. It was actually a danger to liberty he warned against repeatedly.

In his introduction to Destutt de Tracy's Treatise on the Will, Jefferson wrote,

"To take from one because it is thought that his own industry and that of his father's has acquired too much, in order to spare to others, who, or whose fathers have not exercised equal industry and skill, is to violate arbitrarily the first principle of association--'the guarantee to every one of a free exercise of his industry and the fruits acquired by it."[10]

In his 2nd Inaugural Address, he said,

"…that our wish, as well as theirs, is, that the public efforts may be directed honestly to the public good, that peace be cultivated, civil and religious liberty unassailed, law and order preserved; equality of rights maintained, *and that state of property, equal or unequal, which results to every man from his own industry, or that of his fathers.*"[11] [italics added]

Jefferson not only recognizes property rights as "the first principle of association," but clearly speaks to the injustice of social programs that represent a government-enforced redistribution of wealth.   This is not an indictment of compassion. He does not condemn charity or people voluntarily giving aid to the needy.   He condemns the use of government force to confiscate an individual's property, even for the purposes of giving it to someone in need. Regardless of good intentions, this is a clear violation of the non-aggression principle.

Obviously, Jefferson did not recognize achieving "economic equality" as a proper goal of government.[12] Jefferson recognized that a free society that protects equal rights can never result in economic equality. Some would always do better than others. However, respect for each individual's rights gives everyone equal opportunity.

Seventy-four years after the American Revolution, French economist and philosopher Frederic Bastiat wrote a powerful essay called "The Law" to try to convince his fellow countrymen to reject the socialism that was quickly becoming the dominant political philosophy in his own country. He returned directly to the ideas on property rights expressed by Locke and our founding fathers and came to the same conclusions that they did. In these passages, the reader will find familiar themes,

"The law is the organization of the natural right of lawful defense. It is the substitution of a common force for individual forces. And this common force is to do only what the individual forces have a natural and lawful right to do: to protect persons, liberties, and properties; to maintain the right of each, and to cause justice to reign over us all."[13]

Regarding government going beyond this purpose, Bastiat writes,

"But, unfortunately, law by no means confines itself to its proper functions. And when it has exceeded its proper functions, it has not done so merely in some inconsequential and debatable matters. The law has gone further than this; it has acted in direct opposition to its own purpose. The law has been used to destroy its own objective: It has been applied to annihilating the justice that it was supposed to maintain; to limiting and destroying rights which its real purpose was to respect. The law has placed the collective force at the disposal of the unscrupulous who wish, without risk, to exploit the person, liberty, and property of others. It has converted plunder into a right, in order to protect plunder. And it has converted lawful defense into a crime, in order to punish lawful defense."[14]

Like Locke, Jefferson, and other founding fathers, Bastiat eloquently expressed the idea that government cannot go beyond its prime purpose without defeating that purpose. He also introduces the concept of "legal plunder," which is his name for all wealth redistributed by the force of government, instead of by voluntary consent through free trade. Like Jefferson, Bastiat recognizes that this is a fundamental violation of the most basic rights, unjustifiable no matter how noble the intentions. In response to a contemporary advocate of socialism, Bastiat writes,

"Mr. de Lamartine once wrote to me thusly: 'Your doctrine is only the half of my program. You have stopped at liberty; I go on to fraternity.' I answered him: 'The second half of your program will destroy the first.'

In fact, it is impossible for me to separate the word fraternity from the word voluntary. I cannot possibly understand how fraternity can be legally enforced without liberty being legally destroyed, and thus justice being legally trampled underfoot."[15]

There is one thing every philosopher in the liberal tradition makes clear. If one's property is forcefully taken from him without his consent, even for the purposes of providing needed benefits to others, he is not free. Whatever they may think of global warming, this is the "inconvenient truth" that no politician wants to acknowledge.

Sadly, this may very well be the reader's first exposure to these concepts. Our school system no longer instructs our children in them, if they ever did. A common reaction against the ideas presented here is that, while liberty is a noble idea that may have worked in 1776, it is just not practical to talk about society in the 21st century without social programs. This is based upon the assumption that these programs actually provide more health care for their beneficiaries instead of less, a higher quality of life in retirement, and more opportunity for the poor. We will see in a later chapter that exactly the opposite is true. Startling as it may seem, these programs actually diminish the amount of goods and services available even to the poorest of society and ensure a lower quality of life for retirees. Once this economic reality is understood, the fallacy of liberty being "impractical" collapses.

Often, attacking socialism is perceived as an argument against the poor on behalf of the rich, but this is also untrue. Just as legal plunder is perpetrated by what Bastiat would call "false philanthropists," it is similarly perpetrated by corporate interests. In 2008, the entire American financial industry was bailed out by the U.S. Treasury and Federal Reserve to the tune of hundreds of billions of dollars. These subsidies to corporations that should be allowed to fail and be replaced by competitors who perform better is no less a violation of property rights. As with the social programs, the rightful property of one individual is taken by force and redistributed to another.

It doesn't stop with corporate welfare or welfare for the poor. While the numbers for these are enormous, the numbers for Social Security and Medicare are absolutely staggering. The programs currently cost over $1 trillion per year and have unfunded liabilities in the tens or hundreds of trillions of dollars, depending upon whose accounting you use.

Again, Bastiat pierces to the heart of the matter in The Law,

"It is absolutely necessary that this question of legal plunder should be determined, and there are only three solutions of it:

1. When the few plunder the many.

2. When everybody plunders everybody.

3. When nobody plunders anybody.

Partial plunder, universal plunder, absence of plunder, amongst these we have to make our choice. The law can only produce one of these results."[17]

The poor and the rich are both small percentages of society. Programs designed to benefit them would fall under Bastiat's first societal scenario where "the few plunder the many." Social Security and Medicare are paid to virtually everyone. They represent his 2nd scenario, where "everybody plunders everybody." Only by eliminating both practices is the third scenario possible: Nobody plunders anybody. Only then is a society truly free.

As important as property rights are, they are not the only rights. Other essential rights are vital to protecting the central right of self-preservation. These include those enumerated in the Bill of Rights, but one should not think of that short list of constitutional amendments as the length and breadth of our rights. Rather, they are a bare minimum list of protections against government intrusion. In keeping with Locke and our founding fathers, we should remember that in a free society, the people should be able to do anything they wish to, as long as they do not violate the rights of another person. Unfortunately, the vast majority of our laws represent violations of our rights, rather than protection of them.

This is partly caused by expecting government to "prevent crime." While government's core purpose is to punish crimes after they occur, it is quite a different thing for government to try to prevent its citizens from having the opportunity to commit a crime. Once the government sets out to prevent crime, it begins violating rights. The litmus test is the ability to identify a victim of the activity in question. If a law prohibits activity that constitutes aggression against person or property, then it is just. If it does not, then the law is unjust and it is government that is the aggressor.

Consider gun control laws. Clearly, laws against initiating violence (violence not in self-defense) are just and necessary. They protect the right to life. However, there is no victim involved in the mere possession of a firearm, no matter where it is carried or what caliber the bullets. The weapon can be carried into shopping malls, into church, or into a public park. No one is harmed by this activity. It is only when that weapon is used in aggression that legal prohibition is justified.

Prohibiting the possession of weapons clearly violates the ancient right to bear arms, specifically protected by the 2nd Amendment. Even limitations or qualifications on possession of firearms represents a shift from recognizing bearing arms as a right to regarding it as a privilege. Privileges are granted by government and subject to limitation or revocation. Rights are inalienable. They transcend government and are not subject to limitation or revocation. The purpose of the law is to protect them, not attack them. Rights are absolute. Either you have them or you don't.

Again, the issue of practicality is often raised on this subject. Certainly there would be more violence in a society where the citizens' right to bear arms was least restricted. Isn't this true of the United States, where there is more violence than in other countries that more strictly control possession of firearms?

In a word, no. First, the United States is not the most liberal nation, even among nations of the west, in terms of respecting the right to bear arms. As just one example, Switzerland requires that every male between twenty and thirty years of age keep an assault rifle in his home, in order to fulfill his duty to serve in the militia. Anyone who has traveled to Switzerland will attest to the prevalence of guns in their society. It is not uncommon to see young men walking the streets or stopping at the store on their way home from work with an assault rifle strapped across their back. These are not men actively serving in the military, but merely carrying their weapons as part of their everyday lives. Shooting is a huge national pastime in Switzerland, much more so than in America.

Second, there is no empirical proof that prohibiting gun ownership decreases violent crime. In fact, most studies show that violence is the highest in areas where gun control is the strictest. Switzerland is arguably the most liberal western nation in terms of gun ownership. Guns are ubiquitous there. Yet, the per capita gun violence rate is so low that the Swiss don't even bother to track it! [18]

The founders recognized that the right to bear arms was essential to the liberty of the people. It allowed them to take personal responsibility for defense of their persons. Regardless of the responsiveness of the local police, there is no way they can help you at the moment you are attacked. As many have pointed out, all they can do is to take pictures of your body when they arrive at the crime scene. As Switzerland's example demonstrates, an armed citizenry has much less to fear from violent criminals than an unarmed one.

The founders also realized that an armed citizenry would be less likely to be oppressed by their government. Recently, there have been arguments made that the 2nd Amendment was only meant to guarantee the right to bear arms to members of a militia. Others, including the Supreme Court, have attempted to limit or qualify the right to bear arms to particular purposes, such as hunting or defense against criminals. However, the words of the founders could not be clearer on the primary reason to guard the right to bear arms so jealously.

"Before a standing army can rule, the people must be disarmed; as they are in almost every kingdom in Europe. The supreme power in America cannot enforce unjust laws by the sword; because the whole body of the people are armed, and constitute a force superior to any band of regular troops that can be, on any pretence, raised in the United States. A military force, at the command of Congress, can execute no laws, but such as the people perceive to be just and constitutional; for they will possess the power, and jealousy will instantly inspire the inclination, to resist the execution of a law which appears to them unjust and oppressive."[19]

It was no accident that the American Revolutionary War broke out when the British army attempted to disarm the citizens (that's why the British marched to Concord). They recognized that this would leave them defenseless against tyranny. While no one advocates solving most problems with guns, the true purpose of the Second Amendment must be understood. There is no freedom if the government disarms the people.

Another example of victimless crime is the prohibition of certain drugs. However much one may disapprove of drugs that debilitate the mind or body, one certainly is not victimized when somebody else uses them. It is sometimes argued that drug use leads to other crimes such as robbery or assault. However, it is not necessary to prohibit drug use for these reasons. If a drug user commits a robbery, he is subject to prosecution for robbery like any other criminal. If the drug user does not violate anyone else's rights, then there is no justification to use force against him.

From a more practical perspective, the prohibition of alcohol clearly showed that this type of law results in more crime, not less. For some reason, we have ignored this clear lesson and subjected ourselves to all of the same problems with the prohibition of narcotics that we suffered with the prohibition of alcohol. Any rational person can see that the lion's share of the violence associated with drugs is perpetrated by rival gangs or other criminal organizations that are enriched and empowered by prohibition. Certainly there are cases where a drug user commits a robbery or other crime in order to obtain money to purchase drugs. But even this is a result of prohibition. If the drugs weren't illegal, their supply would not be as limited, providing them would not pose such high risk, and their price would be a fraction of what it is today. The motivation for crime for both users and suppliers would be gone.

While these arguments are traditionally associated with one political party or another, party platforms aren't their source. They merely represent a logical application of the non-aggression principle. There are many things other people do that we may not like or think is in their best interests. However, we do not have any legitimate authority to force them to behave in a manner we approve of. We only have a right to defend ourselves against them if they attempt to harm us. This is the essence of liberty. We either live by these principles or resign ourselves that we cannot be allowed to be free. There is no third choice.

Drugs and guns are high profile issues that provide examples of where crime prevention necessarily infringes upon rights. However, crime prevention laws are far more pervasive then this.

For example, there is a law that requires all cash transactions of $10,000 or more to be reported to the federal government. This is supposedly to ensure the transaction does not involve the sale of illegal drugs, money laundering, or some other crime. This is a clear violation of individual rights. Purchasing an automobile with $11,000 in cash, doesn't harm anyone. Yet the government treats you as a criminal until you prove you are not. One is supposed to be presumed innocent until proven guilty according to a principle we say we cherish. Here the law violates that principle.

Most of our laws fail this basic test. This could not be truer for the federal government's network of regulatory agencies. The vast majority of regulations imposed upon commerce by the FDA, the SEC, the FCC, and the host of other agencies are regulations that attempt to prevent crime. By dictating the way in which a certain business activity will be conducted, they attempt to eliminate the opportunity for criminal activity to take place. However, the actions prohibited by most of the regulations are not crimes themselves, and thus violate the right to liberty that government is supposed to protect. This ocean of regulations is also profoundly destructive to the economy.

Gay marriage is another high profile issue. By now, it is probably abundantly clear how the principles of liberty would apply to this "dilemma." Certainly, there is no victim involved in the case of two adults of the same sex deciding to enter a sexual or domestic relationship, whether they call it marriage, cohabitation, partnership, or anything else. As both parties are acting voluntarily, they do not need to be protected from each other, and they certainly are not violating the rights of anyone else. There are many people who find the practice of homosexuality distasteful, and they are fully within their rights to think whatever they like. However, they certainly have no right to use the threat of violence to prevent people from being homosexual.

To be fair, a large percentage of the people arguing against gay marriage do not advocate denying the rights of homosexual people to be homosexual, but rather are against the official recognition of gay marriage by the state. While an argument on religious grounds would not hold water in a free society, there is a practical argument that is at least worth examination.

Official recognition of gay marriage by the government is going to result in a new set of beneficiaries of entitlement benefits. In addition to the beneficiaries themselves, Medicare and Social Security benefits are also paid to surviving spouses. If surviving gay partners are not recognized as spouses, they are not entitled to those benefits when their partners pass away. By legalizing gay marriage, there will be millions of new beneficiaries drawing benefits from entitlement programs that are already financially insolvent. The most lucid argument against gay marriage is on the grounds that society simply cannot afford it.

Certainly, the answer is not to limit the number or type of people that are allowed to get married. The non-aggression principle certainly would not lead one to conclude that heterosexual people are entitled to legal plunder but homosexual people are not. A free society would recognize that nobody is so entitled. However, while society extends these privileges to heterosexual people, they must be extended equally to all members of society.

These are only a few examples of thousands of laws against victimless crimes. While one might be tempted to think that most of these examples don't apply to them, that's a dangerous position to take. History shows that once freedom is lost for a small minority in society, it is lost to the whole. Every one of these examples demonstrates the same principle; when government goes beyond protecting life, liberty, and property, it must necessarily attack life, liberty, and property. In the words of Bastiat, "A citizen cannot at the same time be free and not free."[20]

Of course, the government's activities do not end at the nation's borders. Almost one third of all federal spending goes towards the military. In addition to massive spending on what amounts to a worldwide standing army, the United States has been involved in active wars in the Middle East for over a decade since September 11, 2001. Those wars cost money and lives, which cannot be quantified in dollars and cents.

Many argue for the current wars in the Middle East based upon the low number of U.S. casualties. This completely ignores the casualties on the other side, as well as the massive civilian casualties. The fundamental question is "why did they die?" Even one death is too many in a war that does not have to be fought. When is military force justified? When should it not?

The answers to these questions are relatively simple. The role of government in dealing with other nations is identical to the role of government within its own borders. Its purpose is to defend the life, liberty, and property of its citizens, in this case against aggression by foreign nations. The non-aggression principle applies to other nations just as it does to other citizens. The government has no right to commit acts of aggression, only to defend.

The founders considered the greatest threat to the liberty of the people to reside in the government's war powers, which is why they were so severely limited. The Constitution reserves the power to declare war to Congress, the direct representatives of the people. It also grants Congress the exclusive authority to raise armies, and only for two years at a time, ensuring that a congressional election precedes every new resolution to maintain a standing military force. The founders clearly wanted the decision to go to war and to continue to be at war to be solely in the hands of the people. Only in the face of the most immediate threat did they wish for a standing army to exist.

Today, the United States has military bases in over 130 countries.[21] We are involved in two wars with countries that could not in their wildest dreams successfully invade the United States. We have justified involvement in these wars as a response to terrorist attacks against the United States. Is that justification enough? If the rights of the individual take priority over the needs of the state, how do we determine if the danger is great enough to go to war?

In the next chapter, we will explore the nature of war, what it meant to our founders, and how their ideas apply to the 21st century. The United States currently spends more on defense than the next ten industrialized nations *combined*. Certainly, the expenditure itself violates property rights if unnecessary. However, the most important expenditure is the loss of human life. Only immediate danger can justify it. Our founders knew this, but do we?

In a free society, the people are not servants of their government. Government is their servant. The lives of the people do not belong to the government, nor are the people duty-bound to participate in unnecessary war. War powers are granted to government by the people strictly for the purpose of defending their rights against foreign nations that threaten to take them away. War is meant to be a last resort before the nation is conquered or destroyed by another. This is the level to which the threat must rise before elected representatives have the legitimate authority to commit their constituents to war.

The role of government is to protect the individual rights of its citizens, including the rights to life, liberty, and property; to enforce the non-aggression principle against those who would violate it using coercion, fraud or breach of contract. By attempting to do anything more, government violates the very rights it exists to protect, both in domestic and foreign policy.

No compromise of this limit on government power allows a society to remain free.

Chapter 4
The State of War

"No Nation could preserve its freedom in the midst of continual warfare"

– James Madison[1]

The role of government regarding war powers is the same as it is regarding domestic governance: to defend the life, liberty, and property of the people. Therefore, government may only go to war when the rights of the people have been attacked. Committing its people to war or military action for any other reason is an act of aggression against both the foreign nation it has attacked as well as its own people. That is why the war powers granted in the Constitution are so carefully limited.

With well over a million men and women in uniform, 700 military bases in 130 countries around the world, and a defense budget exceeding $800 billion dollars, it is hard to imagine that the founders did everything they could to prevent the existence of an army during peacetime at all! But they did. Even today, these Constitutional limits are still in place. Regarding war powers, Article I Section 8 of the Constitution allows Congress,

"To declare War, grant Letters of Marque and Reprisal, and make Rules concerning Captures on Land and Water;

To raise and support Armies, but no Appropriation of Money to that Use shall be for a longer Term than two Years;

To provide and maintain a Navy;

To make Rules for the Government and Regulation of the land and naval Forces;

To provide for calling forth the Militia to execute the Laws of the Union, suppress Insurrections and repel Invasions;

To provide for organizing, arming, and disciplining, the Militia, and for governing such Part of them as may be employed in the Service of the United States, reserving to the States respectively, the Appointment of the Officers, and the Authority of training the Militia according to the discipline prescribed by Congress;[2]

The U.S. Army, Navy, and other armed forces, which most people consider institutions as perpetual as the Post Office, have only maintained their permanent existence over the past two centuries as a result of consistent votes by Congress to allow them to exist. This is a fundamental right of the people, to form or disband the army. They exercise it through their elected representatives in Congress. The people can disband the armed forces simply by refusing to elect anyone who will not do so.

As with raising an army, the power to declare war upon another nation also rests solely with Congress. While the president is empowered as commander-in-chief of the army in Article II of the Constitution, only Congress may declare war. This power is widely misunderstood in America today.

Why Must We Declare War?

In May of 2003, the United States invaded Iraq without a formal declaration of war. While there was spirited debate about the justification for the invasion, there was relatively little discussion about the lack of a formal declaration of war by Congress. When brought up by strict constitutionalists, supporters of the war cite H.J. Res. 114 (October 16, 2002), wherein Congress authorized the use of military force. The substance of the argument boils down to, "Congress authorized the president to use military force, so what is the difference between that and a declaration of war?"

There is a drastic difference between a declaration of war and an authorization to use force. The former is the rightful defense of liberty by a free people, and the latter the unjustified initiation of aggression by an autocratic state. The implications reach to the very heart of our republic, calling into question our morality, our freedom, and our national sovereignty.

While war is popularly thought of as the active use of military force, the battles, skirmishes, airstrikes, invasions, etc.; these are not the essence of war. Rather, there is a *state of war*, separate from the actual fighting, that was clearly defined by the Enlightenment philosophers. This "state of war" must exist before military force is justified.

Locke devotes an entire chapter to the state of war in his *Second Treatise*. In it, he writes,

"Men living together according to reason, without a common superior on earth, with authority to judge between them, is properly the state of nature. But force, or a declared design of force, upon the person of another, where there is no common superior on earth to appeal to for relief, is the state of war: and it is the want of such an appeal gives a man the right of war even against an aggressor, tho' he be in society and a fellow subject."[3]

According to Locke, the state of war can arise by an aggressor either using force or declaring the intention to use force. In either case, the relationship between the two parties has changed from a state of nature, or a state of civil society to a state of war. This state or relationship exists totally apart from the physical act of fighting. Military action is actually a result of the state of war. The use of force is only justified in defense, in response to a state of war. Locke also writes,

"This makes it lawful for a man to kill a thief, who has not in the least hurt him, nor declared any design upon his life, any farther than, by the use of force, so to get him in his power, as to take away his money, or what he pleases, from him; because using force, where he has no right, to get me into his power, let his pretence be what it will, I have no reason to suppose, that he, who would take away my liberty, would not, when he had me in his power, take away everything else. And therefore it is lawful for me to treat him as one who has put himself into a state of war with me, i.e. kill him if I can; for to that hazard does he justly expose himself, whoever introduces a state of war, and is aggressor in it."[4]

Other Enlightenment writers also view the state of war as a condition, or a relationship separate from any tangible use of force.[5] Thomas Hobbes writes,

"For war consisteth not in battle only, or the act of fighting, but in a tract of time, wherein the will to contend by battle is sufficiently known: and therefore the notion of time is to be considered in the nature of war, as it is in the nature of weather. For as the nature of foul weather lieth not in a shower or two of rain, but in an inclination thereto of many days together: so the nature of war consisteth not in actual fighting, but in the known disposition thereto during all the time there is no assurance to the contrary. All other time is peace."[6]

Regarding conquests, Jean Jacques Rousseau also recognizes that the state of war is a condition or relationship between two parties that exists outside of the actual fighting,

"First: because, in the first case, the right of conquest, being no right in itself, could not serve as a foundation on which to build any other; the victor and the vanquished people still remained with respect to each other in the state of war, unless the vanquished, restored to the full possession of their liberty, voluntarily made choice of the victor for their chief."[7]

Interestingly, Rousseau argues here that the state of war can continue after the fighting has ceased, as in his example of a conquered people still under the power of their conqueror.

Clearly, the Enlightenment philosophers recognized the state of war as a condition or relationship between two parties, distinct from the martial actions the parties take as a result. The state of war begins with the use of force or the declared intention to use force by an aggressor and gives the other party the right to use lethal force to defend itself. The use of force is justified when a man or a nation recognizes that an aggressor has initiated a state of war against him or it.[8] The state of war can also persist after the fighting ceases, if the conditions which created it still exist.

This was the context in which the framers gave Congress the power to declare war. It was not the power to initiate a war, but the power to officially recognize that a state of war exists. This justifies military action. This interpretation is supported by every request by a United States president for Congress to declare war, and every resolution by Congress to do so. James Madison was the first to request a declaration of war. In his request, he said,

"We behold, in fine, on the side of Great Britain a state of war against the United States, and on the side of the United States a state of peace toward Great Britain."[9]

Congress' resolution declaring war upon Great Britain in 1812 reads,

"Be it enacted by the Senate and House of Representatives of the United States of America in Congress assembled, That war be and the same is hereby declared to exist between the United Kingdom of Great Britain and Ireland and the dependencies thereof, and the United States of America and their territories; and that the President of the United States is hereby authorized to use the whole land and naval force of the United States to carry the same into effect, and to issue private armed vessels of the United States commissions or letters of marque and general reprisal, in such form as he shall think proper, and under the seal of the United States, against the vessels, goods, and effects of the government of the said United Kingdom of Great Britain and Ireland, and the subjects thereof."[10]

Here we find a clear distinction between the state of war and the commencement of the use of military force. Similarly, when James Polk asked Congress to declare war on Mexico in 1846, he said,

"But now, after reiterated menaces, Mexico has passed the boundary of the United States, has invaded our territory and shed American blood upon the American soil. She has proclaimed that hostilities have commenced, and that the two nations are now at war.

As war exists, and, notwithstanding all our efforts to avoid it, exists by the act of Mexico herself, we are called upon by every consideration of duty and patriotism to vindicate with decision the honor, the rights, and the interests of our country. . . .

In further vindication of our rights and defense of our territory, I invoke the prompt action of Congress to recognize the existence of the war, and to place at the disposition of the Executive the means of prosecuting the war with vigor, and thus hastening the restoration of peace."[11]

The official declaration reads,

"Whereas, by the act of the Republic of Mexico, a state of war exists between that Government and the United States: Be it enacted by the Senate and House of Representatives of the United States of American in Congress assembled, That for the purpose of enabling the government of the United States to prosecute said war to a speedy and successful termination..."[12]

All subsequent presidential requests and Congressional declarations of war support that a state of war existed before the United States commenced planned military operations. In each case, the president makes his case for why the enemy nation has been the aggressor and why he believes a state of war already exists. He then requests that Congress formally declare it. In requesting a declaration of war with Spain, President William McKinley stated,

"I now recommend the adoption of a joint resolution declaring that a state of war exists between the United States of America and the Kingdom of Spain, that the definition of the international status of the United States as a belligerent power may be made known and the assertion of all its rights in the conduct of a public war may be assured."[13]

Congress' official declaration not only recognizes that the war already exists, but actually specifies the date on which the state of war commenced,

"Be it enacted by the Senate and House of Representatives of the United States of America in Congress assembled, First. That war be, and the same is hereby declared to exist, and that war has existed since the twenty-first day of April, anno Domini eighteen hundred and ninety-eight, including said day, between the United States of American and the Kingdom of Spain."[14]

Here, not only does Congress recognize that a state of war already existed before the onset of planned military operations, but actually indicates the exact day on which the state of war began, taking the time to specify "including said day," so that no mistake can be made about when the two nations entered a state of war.

When President Wilson requested a declaration of war against Germany in 1917, he said,

"...I advise that the Congress declare the recent course of the Imperial German government to be in fact nothing less than war against the government and people of the United States; that it formally accept the status of belligerent which has thus been thrust upon it; and that it take immediate steps, not only to put the country in a more thorough state of defense but also to exert all its power and employ all its resources to bring the government of the German Empire to terms and end the war."[15]

The official declaration reads,

"Whereas the Imperial German Government has committed repeated acts of war against the Government and the people of the United States of America: Therefore be it Resolved by the Senate and House of Representatives of the United States of America in Congress assembled, That the state of war between the United States and the Imperial German Government which has been thrust upon the United States is hereby formally declared; and that the President be, and he is hereby, authorized and directed to employ the entire naval and military forces..."[16]

Notice that Congress emphasizes not only the existence of a state of war, but that it has been "thrust upon" the United States by acts of war committed by Germany. The declaration takes pains to officially identify Germany as the aggressor.

Finally, in President Roosevelt's request for a declaration of war on Japan, he says,

"I ask that the Congress declare that since the unprovoked and dastardly attack by Japan on Sunday, December 7th, 1941, a state of war has existed between the United States and the Japanese empire."[17]

In response, Congress resolves,

"Whereas the Imperial Government of Japan has committed unprovoked acts of war against the Government and the people of the United States of America: Therefore be it Resolved by the Senate and House of Representatives of the United States of America in Congress assembled, That the state of war between the United States and the Imperial Government of Japan which has thus been thrust upon the United States is hereby formally declared; and the President is hereby authorized and directed to employ the entire naval and military forces of the United States and the resources of the Government to carry on war against the Imperial Government of Japan; and, to bring the conflict to a successful termination, all of the resources of the country are hereby pledged by the Congress of the United States."[18]

After the United States declared war on Japan, Germany declared war on the United States. The United States responded by declaring war on Germany, consistent with Locke's premise that a state of war exists once an aggressor declares his intent to initiate force.

Every declaration of war in U.S. history demonstrates the principle that a state of war must exist *before* planned military action is justified. That state of war exists only if there was some previous act of war by that country against the United States.

It is equally important to note that in each case where a president requested a declaration of war, he preceded his request with a statement of the overt acts or the formal declarations of the aggressor nation that supported his belief that a state of war existed.

What relevance does this have to the invasion of Iraq and other military operations the United States has undertaken without a declaration of war?

First, there is a moral question. Was the invasion of Iraq justified? In the five wars the United States fought under a formal declaration of war, the justification was based upon a president "making a case" that a state of war already existed between the United States and the nation in question. The president presented evidence, in the form of a list of overt acts or a declaration by the aggressor nation, supporting his claim that a state of war existed. Congress then deliberated on the evidence and cast a vote that supported a formal declaration that the United States was already at war. Certainly, the justifications for the declared wars can be disputed. However, the fact remains that both the executive and legislative branches followed a constitutional process that was far more than a formality or vestige left over from earlier, courtlier ages. It was a process that was directly accountable to the people through their elected representatives in Congress.

With the wars in Iraq and Afghanistan, as in the Korean and Viet Nam wars, that process did not occur. Regarding the Iraq War, the debate shifted away from whether or not a state of war existed to whether or not Iraq posed a threat to the security of the United States. This debate was irrelevant. No interpretation of the Enlightenment philosophy or of the U.S. Constitution justifies military action merely on the basis of another nation representing a threat. As it did in the Korean and Viet Nam wars, the government used military force when no state of war existed, thereby becoming, by definition, the aggressor.

Obviously, President Bush would not have been able to request a declaration of war with Iraq. There were no overt acts of aggression by Iraq against the United States for him to cite as his evidence of a state of war. Neither was there a declaration by Iraq of their intention to use force against the United States. In fact, Saddam Hussein repeatedly denied his country's possession of weapons of mass destruction and invited President Bush to a conference in an attempt to avoid military conflict. Hussein all but declared a state of "non-war" with the United States. So, there was no case to be made for a state of war based upon a declaration by an aggressor. Had the United States government held itself to the standard set by the Constitution and close to two hundred years of precedent, there would have been no Iraq War. The same can be said for the Korean War, the Viet Nam war, Grenada, Bosnia, Somalia, etc.

Rousseau's insights shed a different light on the post-invasion "insurgency" as well. Rousseau said the state of war continues to exist even after the cessation of fighting until "the vanquished, restored to the full possession of their liberty, voluntarily made choice of the victor for their chief." According to this argument, the Iraqi insurgents have every right to go on killing Americans, their conqueror, until they are both restored to full possession of their liberty and have voluntarily chosen the United States, or the government that the United States installs, as their rightful government. We have seen similar results in two previous, undeclared wars. In Viet Nam, we left in disgrace. In Korea, we are still there, almost sixty years later. Perhaps there is a correlation between moral force and success.

There is also a sovereignty question related to this issue. Since the establishment of the United Nations, the United States has not declared war. Yet, its government has been almost continuously involved in military operations, usually under the auspices of U.N. resolutions. Another passage in Locke may speak directly to this.

"To avoid this state of war (wherein there is no appeal but to heaven, and wherein every the least difference is apt to end, where there is no authority to decide between the contenders) is one great reason of men's putting themselves into society, and quitting the state of nature: for where there is an authority, a power on earth, from which relief can be had by appeal, there the continuance of the state of war is excluded, and the controversy is decided by that power."[19]

Do American legislators still recognize their own power to declare war? Or do they recognize the United Nations as a world governing power, believing there is now "an authority, a power on earth, from which relief can be had by appeal?" While one might be inclined to think it beneficial to have a world governing body that can "referee" between nations that would otherwise make war upon each other, one must remember what a surrender of sovereignty means. The United Nations' "Universal Declaration of Human Rights" does not recognize the same limits on government power that our own Bill of Rights does. If the United States is no longer a sovereign nation, but merely a subsidiary of a world government, then that government's laws hold precedence over U.S. laws. While we cannot lose our natural rights, they can be violated by governments, regardless of them being inalienable to us.

Although merely speculation, this is one possible explanation for why the United States has failed to declare war upon another nation since the United Nations was founded, while almost continually involved in military operations during the same period. If this is truly the position of our legislators, then they are violating their oath to defend the Constitution.

Undeclared wars also have implications for liberty. The founders delegated war powers out of recognized necessity. They lived, as we do, in a world where an aggressor nation could threaten the security of even a free, non-aggressive state. However, they granted those powers for the specific purpose of defense against aggression. The declaration of war process provided a litmus test of whether or not military action was justified.

It is not just the soldiers that war places at risk. Indeed, civilian casualties in Iraq far outweigh those of soldiers on either side. In the past, the United States has been insulated from civilian casualties because of its remoteness from the countries in which it has waged war. However, the 21st century has already shown us that remoteness no longer provides that insulation. Given the direct risk to U.S. citizens that accompanies war, should the United States government be allowed to wage an undeclared war? Are a people really free when they can be put at risk and into debt by their government in the absence of a true state of war?

Obviously, the answer to both of these questions is no. A government that can arbitrarily commit its nation to war or "military police actions" is not the servant of the people, but a tyrannical master, one which can give or take the lives of its citizens for its own reasons. This is beneath even the relationship of a slave to his master.

While the lion's share of media attention is understandably focused upon the active wars in the Middle East, the vast majority of the U.S. military, in dollars and personnel, is invested elsewhere. Over 70% of our military budget is spent on operations not related to the active wars. The United States has military operations in Japan, South Korea, throughout Europe, and in countless other places around the world. Are any of these operations justified?

The answer depends upon whether those troops are deployed in defense against a previous aggression or not. The answer to that question is obvious. No nation has attacked the United States since 1945. Mutual destruction is certainly a possibility in the event of a nuclear war, but armed forces are doing nothing to prevent nuclear war by being deployed overseas. Whether using non-aggression or the Constitution as a standard, our military presence around the world is completely justified.

Some argue the U.S. is defending its allies or "promoting democracy;" that it is defending nations that have democratically elected governments against non-democratically elected governments, or defending a democratic faction in a civil war, such as n South Korea. Today, these are generally accepted as legitimate reasons for military action. It would probably come as quite a surprise to most Americans that our founding fathers specifically warned us against precisely this. In his farewell address to the nation, George Washington stated, "It is our true policy to steer clear of permanent Alliances with any portion of the foreign world."[20]

In his first inaugural address, Thomas Jefferson said,

"About to enter, fellow-citizens, on the exercise of duties which comprehend everything dear and valuable to you, it is proper you should understand what I deem the essential principles of our Government, and consequently those which ought to shape its Administration. I will compress them within the narrowest compass they will bear, stating the general principle, but not all its limitations. Equal and exact justice to all men, of whatever state or persuasion, religious or political; peace, commerce, and honest friendship with all nations, entangling alliances with none…"[21]

Sometimes, military action is justified to "protect our interests" in some foreign land. This is inconsistent with the non-aggression principle, which means using the military only in defense. How could we be fighting "defensively" in another country? Perhaps it would be if the country had initiated aggression or previously attempted to invade the United States, but that hasn't happened since 1775. Cheerleading and nationalism aside, it is clear that no war fought by the United States since at least 1945[22] has been justified.

Our founders recognized that Europe was almost constantly plagued by war, whether between nations or civil wars. Then and now, warfare leads to the bankruptcy of governments and the people themselves. For a self-sufficient nation rooted in non-aggression, there is nothing to be gained and everything to be lost by committing to the protection of other nations.

More importantly, since warfare must be paid for by taxes, which are collected by force, and because warfare results in the loss of life to individual citizens, then unnecessary is a violation of the non-aggression principle by the government against its own people.

What would constitute a real threat to the life, liberty, and property of the people of the United States? It would have to be either a missile or airstrike or an invasion. Both are unlikely due to the United States' vast superiority in military capabilities to almost any other nation.

Obviously, none of the wars we have fought in the past 60 years have been justified by the non-aggression principle or the Constitution. As Madison warned, this cannot be allowed to continue if the people wish to remain free.

Chapter 5
The Economics of Liberty

"...every man, as long as he does not violate the laws of justice, is left perfectly free to pursue his own interests his own way and to bring both his industry and capital into competition with those of other men."

– Adam Smith (1776)[1]

Merriam-Webster defines economics as "a social science concerned chiefly with description and analysis of the production, distribution, and consumption of goods and services."[2] Put more simply, economics is the science of the acquisition and exchange of property. Property is not only one of the most important natural rights, it is the one most often threatened. Violators of property rights often try to separate property from life and liberty, as if either of the three could exist without the other two. Proponents of various "progressive" economic theories are no exception. As with all other questions of human interaction, the non-aggression principle makes the answers to economic questions quite simple. There is only one economic system that does not violate the non-aggression principle: laissez faire capitalism.

That may seem like an odd statement after the most significant economic crisis since the Great Depression, which the whole world seems to be blaming on a *failure* of capitalism. Supposedly, it has been three decades of "deregulation," culminating in the "laissez faire policies of the Bush administration" that caused the massive speculative bubbles in the stock market and real estate that has since threatened to plunge the world into depression.

The Great Depression actually provides historical precedent for our present crisis, although the government's version of the correlation is predictably backwards. According to the government, it was too much freedom that caused the crisis and only massive government intervention can get us out. The truth is exactly the opposite.

However, before we analyze the crisis and whether or not capitalism caused it, we need to define capitalism. Like freedom, there is no shortage of people ready to talk about it, but there is a dearth of people who understand what it really is.

A thorough and scholarly explanation of capitalism is beyond the scope of this book. However, as with the philosophical and political principles examined previously, the economic principles are also relatively simple. The most important is that capitalism is the only economic system in which all of the transactions between people are voluntary. Therefore, it is the only economic system under which people are truly free. The sole purpose of government in a capitalist economic system is to protect property rights. While politicians say economic issues should be treated differently, it is actually even more important that government be limited to this role in regard to economics. Nevertheless, it is here that government commits its most egregious crimes.

To define capitalism, one could look to Adam Smith's seminal "Wealth of Nations."[3] That is not a bad place to start. However, the reader might be surprised that the word "capitalism" appears nowhere in any of its five volumes. Instead, Smith refers to "a system of natural liberty."[4] This is actually as good a definition of capitalism as any! However, Merriam-Webster's definition of capitalism represents the way most economists define it:

"...an economic system characterized by private or corporate ownership of capital goods, by investments that are determined by private decision, and by prices, production, and the distribution of goods that are determined mainly by competition in a free market"[5]

Of the three elements in this definition, private ownership of capital, voluntary exchange, and competition, it is the second that is fundamental to the other two, for two reasons.

First, as long as there is voluntary exchange of property, there will be private ownership of capital. Since all government action is carried out by force, there is no way for government to acquire property in a "voluntary exchange." Even a revenue generating enterprise started by government had to be funded into existence by tax money, which are collected under the threat of force. In a system where all of the transactions are voluntary, all property, including capital goods, remain privately owned.

Second, when all transactions are voluntary, most buyers and sellers will attempt to act in their best interests. Sellers will try to convince buyers to purchase their products or services rather than those of others. Likewise, buyers are going to attempt to find the best products available at the lowest prices. This motivates sellers to maximize their quality and minimize their price so their products will be chosen. Thus, voluntary exchange naturally results in competition.

If what fundamentally defines capitalism is that all transactions are executed by mutual, voluntary consent, then the government's role in a capitalist system is to protect the participants from aggression against their property. That means protecting all parties from force or fraud and enforcing contracts. Capitalism's proponents often focus on the utilitarian argument, that capitalism has historically produced better results than other economic systems. While valid, the moral argument is more important. Contrary to several decades of "progressive" propaganda, capitalism is the *only* morally justifiable economic system, rather than the least justifiable. It is the only system that does not violate the non-aggression principle. It is the economic system of freedom.

As with all other societal questions, freedom is at the root of every economic argument, whether one examines supply, demand, wages, prices, productivity, or efficiency. In a capitalist system, every participant freely chooses whether to buy or sell and at what price, based upon what they believe to be their best interests. If prices for a particular good or service are too high, demand for that product falls and the sellers must lower their prices or not sell the product at all. Therefore, the free choices of buyers and sellers determine the price level. Competition among sellers keeps that price low while still allowing the sellers to make a profit, because customers buy from the seller at the lowest price available when choosing between the same or very similar products. Sellers are also constantly trying to lower their production costs, so they can lower prices further and win business away from competitors. These simple cause and effect relationships that occur in a capitalist system drive supply and quality up and prices down, resulting in a higher standard of living for everyone. They all result from individuals being free to choose what is in their own best interests. Adam Smith called this the "invisible hand."[6]

When government intervenes into the marketplace, this free choice is taken away. That's really what government "economic policy" represents. It is using the threat of violence to force buyers and sellers to make choices they otherwise would not make. No matter how stirring the speech or utopian the vision, this is the reality of government intervention. The first thing that should be apparent is that it is morally repugnant. It also produces disastrous results. Once buyers and sellers are no longer freely choosing based upon their self-interest, the cause and effect relationships that drive up quality and availability and drive prices down cease to exist. The equilibrium that free choice brought to the market is destroyed.

There is a simple lesson in all of this. When people are left alone and their property rights are protected, they will trade with each other to their mutual benefit indefinitely.

Arguably, one of the most laissez faire capitalism systems in history was 19th century America. The economic freedom, both in England and the United States during that century directly resulted in the industrial revolution. For decades, Americans have been taught a destructive myth about this period. They have been taught that the unfettered free market resulted in a diminishing quality of life for the working class, the cruel practice of child labor, and the need for government to "save working people from laissez faire capitalism." Much of government economic policy is still based upon this fiction.

In *The Capitalist Manifesto: The Historic, Economic, and Philosophic Case for Laissez Faire*, Andrew Bernstein argues exactly the opposite. He says that the error is rooted in a lack of historical perspective and failing to look at conditions of the working class before the industrial revolution, which were far worse.

"It is difficult for men in the industrial West today to conceive of the kind of poverty that was widespread in pre-capitalist Europe. By a test employed in Lyons, France, in the 17th century, poverty was reached when daily income was less than the daily cost of minimum bread requirement – in other words, when a person could not make enough money to buy a crust of bread."[7]

Once the official story is discarded, it becomes clear why the working class left their rural occupations for factory work in the city: they were better off doing so. Not only did they make more money working the same or shorter hours, but the mass production and technological advances of the industrial revolution increased the supply of products by large orders of magnitude. With the increase in supply came decreases in the general price levels of goods, or an increase in "real wages."[8] The quality of life of the working class didn't decline during the industrial revolution. It skyrocketed.

Thus, capitalism benefits the poorest segment of society the most, rather than the rich at the expense of the poor. It is for those whose income is smallest that the purchasing power of the money they earn is the most important. We have been led to believe that capitalism involves government protection of the wealthy and large corporations at the expense of the poor and middle classes. The truth is that capitalism protects no one, only the right to trade voluntarily. Some say that such a system leaves some people behind. However, the reality is that the poorest segments of society enjoyed an improving quality of life throughout the 19th century, while their quality of life has deteriorated since government began "reforming capitalism."

Bernstein also dismantles the myth that the industrial revolution was responsible for child labor. Nothing is more associated with the industrial revolution than the image of poor Oliver Twist, the orphan victim of an uncaring industrial England that exploited and abused him. But child labor had been practiced throughout history. The children working in American factories of the 19th Century had much easier work to do there than they had on the farm. More importantly, the industrial revolution resulted in such huge increases in productivity that within 100 years, it was no longer necessary for families to send their children to work. Addressing child labor in England, Bernstein writes,

"Finally, it was only the wealth created by roughly a century of capitalism that ended the age-old necessity for children to work. The percentage of child labor in the textile mills had been declining for decades prior to the years 1835-38, the period in which inspectors began to enforce the Factory Act passed by Parliament in 1833. The figures bear this out. In 1816, children under the age of 10 constituted 6.8 percent of the cotton industry's labor force, but by 1835 a mere 0.3 percent. Children under the age of 13 were an estimated 20 percent of the labor force in 1816, and but 13.1 percent in 1835.

Similarly, there was a decline of those under the age of 18 in those years from 51.2 percent of the labor force to 43.4."[9]

The industrial revolution did not create child labor. It ended it.

While the west has been associated with capitalism over the past century, the east has been associated with socialism or communism. In addition to communism's disastrous failure to achieve prosperity, it also fails the moral test. While some mistakenly believe communism is people "sharing" the goods and services produced by the collective, nothing could be further from the truth. The collective is no more than a society of individuals. Each individual has a right to the fruits of his or her labor. Communism denies this right. Communism says the fruit of the individual's labor belongs to the collective. How does the communist government obtain it for the collective? By seizing it under the threat of violence, like any other government acquisition of property. Communism is nothing more than Bastiat's "everybody plunders everybody" taken to its logical extreme. It constantly violates the non-aggression principle. There is no "sharing" involved in communism. Only plunder.

In order to ensure the stolen property is distributed the way they wish it to be, socialist or communist economies must be centrally planned. Instead of distribution being the result of millions of independent agents making free choices, it is determined by the decisions of a small number of people in the central government. As Hayek demonstrates in *The Road to Serfdom*, there is no way any person or small group can replace the "invisible hand" resulting from all of those independent decisions. In his own words,

"And because all the details of the changes constantly affecting the conditions of demand and supply can never be fully known, or quickly enough be collected and disseminated, by any one centre, what is required is some apparatus of registration which automatically records all the relevant effects of individual actions, and whose indications are at the same time the resultant of, and the guide for, all the individual decisions. This is precisely what the price system does under competition, and which no other system even promises to accomplish."[10]

Like most of Europe, the United States has a "mixed economy," attempting to combine elements of capitalism and socialism to more equally distribute wealth. This includes a "social safety net" for those who are unable to produce enough to meet their own needs.

All of the mixed economies of the west have one thing in common: economic decline. Certainly, there are temporary recoveries here and there by one nation in relation to the others, but the overall quality of life for people in the mixed economies has been diminishing almost from the moment they decided to try to mix socialism with capitalism. Most people do not see the European Union for what it is: a temporary solution for a group of countries that became unable to sustain themselves economically on their own. This was the natural result of the attempt to plunder the more productive members of society to support the less productive. Combining their economies under one currency and centrally planned economy merely allows them to combine the productive capabilities of those citizens in all of their societies and thus create a larger pool to plunder. However, the same forces that caused those nations to fail economically on their own will eventually overcome the group of nations together. There is no reason to expect a different result for the United States.

So far, the United States has been able to avoid the economic collapses of the European economies because it has less outright socialism than its European counterparts. However, the compromises it did make with socialism were the cracks in the foundation. As it has become more and more socialist, those cracks have begun to widen. Now America sits on the edge of the same precipice as the economies of Europe.

A mixed economy has the same moral and economic weaknesses that communism or socialism has. It both violates the non-aggression principle and destroys the productive mechanism of capitalism, which relies on the free, un-coerced decisions of all participants. While some might argue that a mixed economy attempts to combine a moral solution (socialism's "economic equality") with a pragmatic one (capitalism's productivity); this argument is absurd. Trying to achieve either moral or pragmatic results by forcing people to obey under the threat of violence just doesn't work. If there is some transcendent justice in the world, it is that violating the non-aggression principle is never successful in creating a sustainable economy. Only a free people remain self-sufficient.

Mixed economies are also centrally planned, although they leave some choices up to individual buyers and sellers. The planning is accomplished through government interventions into the marketplace, but produce unintended and undesirable results. Even interventions to benefit capitalists, like corporate bailouts, are a socialist aspect of America's mixed economy, not a capitalist one. Heavy regulation over the market is also an aspect of socialism, rather than capitalism, as it prohibits free choices by producers and consumers, regardless of whether those choices represent harm to others.

Socialism is further represented by massive social programs like Medicare, Medicaid, Social Security, and traditional welfare. While Social Security and Medicare are in theory funded by the contributions of the beneficiaries, there is no effective controlling mechanism to distribute benefits proportionately according to contribution, although Social Security has a crude methodology that attempts to do so. In reality, the outlays to today's beneficiaries are not made from their own contributions, but from those who are presently paying into the system. This means these programs are really nothing more than another government wealth redistribution scheme. Most importantly, the participants do not participate voluntarily, but under the coercive power of government.

Property rights are also violated for corporate interests. In an attempt to "manage the economy," public funds are used by the government to bail out failed corporations deemed "too big" or "too important" to be allowed to go bankrupt. This not only violates the rights of the people whose property is confiscated to underwrite the bailouts, but also causes distortions in the economy. The failure of unsound businesses and their replacement by more efficient ones is a natural benefit of a free market.

Rather than a compromise between freedom and slavery, which sounds bad enough, the mixed economy violates liberty more fundamentally. In a mixed economy, the citizens no longer have an inalienable right to their property, but rather the privilege of keeping that property the government doesn't choose to take. Changing property from a right to a privilege crosses the majority of the divide between freedom and slavery.

A mixed economy is not sustainable. In order to fund the massive social programs, the government siphons off the surplus productivity from those producing more than they consume and distributes those savings to those consuming more than they produce. Savings and capital are diminished at first and eventually destroyed, as the incentive to save is eroded. The laborer of today no longer saves for his retirement, partly because he is unable to due to the portion of his income that is seized to pay present beneficiaries, and partly because he knows (or at least believes) that future generations will pay those benefits for him.

One need look no further for proof than the present American economy. After decades of socialist programs like Social Security, Medicare, other government redistribution schemes, heavy regulation and other interventions into the market, the United States has gone from being the world's largest creditor to the world's largest debtor. Both the people and the government are mired in debt, and the economy has a negative savings rate. No longer is the American worker the highest paid or most productive in the world. One by one, the United States has lost its dominance in almost every economic sector, no longer producing the majority of goods and services it consumes. While our politicians may try to lead us to believe economic cycles "just happen," a sober look at the departure we've made from our founding principles reveals the true reason for our economic decline. This departure is rooted in violating property rights and interference with capitalism's invisible hand.

All of this relates directly to the present economic crisis. Was this a failure of capitalism? Was it the supposedly laissez faire policies of the Bush administration that caused the crisis? Is more regulation the answer? Are public works programs, stimulus packages, and government infrastructure projects going to bring us out of this depression?

The government and its economic advisors say they will. This should surprise no one. Even with the best of intentions, government officials naturally want to "do something" about every societal problem that arises. As citizens, we share the responsibility for this in constantly demanding that our government take action against anything in society we find unsatisfactory.

However, if government is supposed to protect life, liberty, and property, then any action by government to interfere with market forces runs contrary to its purpose. For example, the seizure of money from taxpayers to subsidize failing corporations represents aggression by government against the very property it exists to protect. While disastrous from a utilitarian perspective, the more compelling argument against bailouts is a moral one. The government simply does not have the legitimate authority to do it, even if a majority desires it.

Over the past century, two competing schools of thought have emerged in the discipline of economics. The Austrian School of Economics,[11] including Ludwig Von Mises, Friedrich Hayek, Murray Rothbard, and others, generally argue the case for capitalism. The other school consists of followers of John Maynard Keynes, known commonly as Keynesians.[12] Keynesianism has dominated government economic policies for most of the past century.

Keynesians saw the Great Depression as a result of inherent flaws in the capitalist system. They argued that a capitalist society will become so productive and efficient that it will eventually produce more goods than will be demanded by the market, resulting in falling prices and unemployment. For Keynes, falling prices were a problem. He saw the deflation that accompanied the bursting of the 1920's stock market bubble as the problem itself, rather than a consequence of the bubble that preceded it.

Keynes also viewed savings as a problem. For Keynes, excessive savings led to a decrease in consumption, triggering falling prices, over-supply, and unemployment. He called this phenomenon "the Paradox of Thrift."

Based upon these and other perceived "inherent flaws" in free market capitalism, Keynes prescribed government interventions during recessions to rebalance the economy. All of Keynes' solutions were based upon stimulating demand, which would in turn result in stabilization of falling prices and employment of unemployed workers. Keynes believed government spending should take the place of the missing consumer spending. He recommended government run deficits, and institute public works programs to employ unemployed workers. With government replacing the lost demand that accompanied the recession, the economy would be "stimulated" into rebalancing itself.

These ideas should sound very familiar to most Americans. Even if you have never studied economics in school, you have been told all of your life that the health of the economy depends upon "consumer confidence," "price stability," and "access to credit." All of these ideas proceed logically from the Keynesian assumption that demand is the key to wealth-creation.

One should not be surprised that Keynes was a devout socialist. Keynesianism is the economic school of socialism, including the "mixed economy" variety practiced here in the United States. Keynes' economics prescribes a centrally-planned economy, forsaking the free market as incapable of allowing everyone to prosper. It is obvious many of his ideas influenced the policies of FDR. The New Deal can generally be described as Keynesianism put into practice. Despite the Great Depression lasting almost twenty years, history has somehow represented these policies as successful. Of course, this is the official, government-approved history that is taught in our increasingly centrally-controlled public schools. There are plenty of dissenters to this official nonsense, just as there were in Renaissance Europe when most governments officially endorsed the idea that the world was flat.

The Austrian school can be generally understood as having built upon the foundation of the classical economics of Adam Smith, but having improved upon it. Generally, the Austrian school believes that, left to their own without government intervention, individuals would trade freely with each other indefinitely to their mutual benefit.[13]

While Adam Smith is a great place to start to learn about capitalism, one must remember he was writing at a time when "the dismal science" itself was a young science. Opponents of capitalism often pit modern economic theories against Smith's, as if his writing was the last word on capitalism. This is disingenuous. As with Einstein's theories in physics, the basic elements are sound, but the Austrian economists have come a long way since 1776 in developing economic theories about capitalism.[14]

The Austrian school of economics disagrees fundamentally with virtually every aspect of Keynesianism. First and foremost, the Austrian school does not see recessions as spontaneously occurring as a result of inherent flaws in capitalism. They make a compelling argument that recessions are the inevitable corrections that follow periods of monetary inflation by the banking system. They argue that monetary inflation creates distortions in the market, including inflated prices and misallocation of resources. This includes human resources employed in projects that are ultimately not profitable in the long term, but appear so due to an excess supply of money and artificially low interest rates.

Once the inflation-created bubble bursts, market forces immediately begin attempting to correct the imbalances that accompanied it. Thus, asset prices that were artificially inflated due to government manipulation of the money supply and interest rates begin falling to their true market levels. Business ventures that only appeared profitable go bankrupt. Their assets are liquidated and put to more productive use by new managers. People that were employed in unprofitable enterprises must be laid off and allowed to find jobs in truly profitable ventures.

In order to allow this correction to occur with the least economic pain, the Austrian school prescribes maximum flexibility in the labor market. Minimum wages, excessive regulation, and other impediments to people leaving one job and obtaining another can only prolong the crisis. While the Austrian school advocates for laissez faire under any economic conditions, they argue that it is especially important in a recession, so the painful adjustment process takes as little time as possible.

It should be obvious how the two competing ideologies relate to 21st century America. We have just experienced a massive correction in both the housing market and the stock market, following a long period of monetary inflation and artificially low interest rates. The Keynesians argue that there is no cause/effect relationship between the previous monetary inflation and the present correction. Keynesian policy is for government to counter falling prices with increases in the money supply and artificially lower interest rates. They advocate "keeping people employed" if possible and employing those who lose their jobs in public works projects. They believe that only by stimulating demand will the crisis be resolved.

The Austrians prescribe exactly the opposite. Since the "bubble" was created by government creating artificial conditions in the market, the correction must be allowed to occur with all possible haste. They argue housing and stock assets were unsustainably overpriced, and that resisting the natural market forces trying to lower them to their true value will only prolong the crisis. Similarly, resisting market forces to liquidate unprofitable business so that their assets can be reallocated to truly profitable use also prolongs the crisis. Finally, they argue that government attempts to keep people employed in ventures that are ultimately unprofitable is also counterproductive.

Which school is correct? One must answer the questions for oneself. Do you believe wealth and prosperity are created by borrowing and spending or do you believe they are created by production and savings? Do you believe recessions "just happen," as the Keynesians would argue, or do you believe there must be some reason why demand suddenly falls during periods of apparent prosperity? Ultimately, one must ask oneself the crucial question. Do you believe human beings will thrive more in a state of liberty or under government control?

One need not try to answer these questions in a vacuum. Competing theories are often evaluated based upon their ability to predict results. In this respect, there is little doubt as to which theory has more validity. Keynesianism was employed at the start of the Great Depression, first by Herbert Hoover, and then by FDR. Obviously, neither president predicted it would take 11 years for their "solutions" to work or that the "solution" would be World War II.[15] Each president believed his policies would solve the economic problems of the Depression in a relatively short time. None of the Keynesian predictions were accurate, either during the Depression or in the business cycles of subsequent decades.

In contrast, the predictions of the Austrian school are consistently accurate. Both Ludwig Von Mises and Friedrich Hayek predicted the Great Depression while mainstream economists saw no end in sight to the boom of the 1920's. Similarly, while mainstream economists and politicians were telling us the "prosperity" of the housing boom was real, it was a staunch supporter of the Austrian school that predicted the economic crisis we find ourselves in today.

Despite years of being ridiculed (sometimes outright laughed at) during appearances on financial shows, Peter Schiff of Euro Pacific Capital repeatedly warned that the apparent prosperity accompanying the housing bubble was an illusion, and that our economy had serious fundamental flaws that would result in an economic cataclysm. Written in 2006 and published in February of 2007, Schiff's book *Crash Proof: How to Benefit from the Coming Economic Collapse*[16] accurately predicted the bursting of the housing bubble, the stock market correction, and the ensuing government efforts to combat the economic consequences. There is also a video compilation of Schiff's 2006 television appearances titled "Peter Schiff was Right" circulating the internet. The video shows Schiff making his accurate predictions of the 2008 crisis years in advance, accompanied by peals of laughter from other panelists who derisively nick-named him "Dr. Doom." Obviously, the laughter has now subsided.

Schiff was not able to make those predictions based upon supernatural powers. He made them based upon sound theory, the theory of the Austrian school of economics. He is currently appearing on nationally televised financial shows arguing the Austrian position to let the free market correct the imbalances which were caused by the monetary expansion of the past decade. In keeping with the Austrian school, Schiff recognizes that resources have been grossly misallocated by this bubble, and must be allowed to be reallocated. Unprofitable businesses must be allowed to go bankrupt so their assets can be liquidated and put to profitable use. Housing and stock prices must be allowed to fall to their natural market levels, as they have been artificially inflated by monetary expansion. Workers must be laid off from unprofitable companies and allowed to find jobs in ventures that are profitable and therefore sustainable in the long term.

Despite his accurate predictions in the past, Schiff's recommendations are being ignored by government policy makers. Every action government has taken so far contradicts the solutions proposed by Schiff and the Austrians, agreeing instead with the Keynesians. Government has not allowed unprofitable businesses to go bankrupt so their assets can be put to productive use. They have used massive public funds, in violation of property rights, to keep these unprofitable businesses operating. The latest example is the bailout package for the automakers. Government is similarly trying to resist the natural adjustment of housing prices by inflating the money supply and forcing interest rates close to zero. This is an attempt to re-inflate the housing bubble, which the Austrians predict will be unsuccessful but will prolong the painful period of adjustment.

President Obama has continually pushed the legislature for massive government projects, including huge "infrastructure projects." All of this proceeds from Keynesian ideas about government stimulating demand and achieving "full employment." It ignores the violation of property rights that occurs each time the government uses tax money for anything other than protecting life, liberty, and property. It also contradicts the Austrian school's theory that these government "solutions" merely make the crisis worse.

The Great Depression provides a historical precedent to the present crisis. Let us consider some of the similarities.

First, the Great Depression began following a period of massive monetary expansion of the currency. The Austrian school points to this as the reason for the stock market bubble that burst in 1929. Then, as now, a Republican president was in office when the crisis began. Herbert Hoover was also a president whom history inaccurately blames for being "too laissez faire." However, it was not the free market that caused the bubble. It was this expansion of the money supply, an interference with the free market that caused it.[17]

Like George Bush, once the crisis started, Hoover was a massive interventionist. Many of the New Deal programs Roosevelt introduced were really recreations of Hoover policies on a much larger scale. As we will discuss later, it was Hoover's attempts to interfere with the free market correction that turned the 1929 recession in the Great Depression. As Murray Rothbard wrote in *America's Great Depression*,

"President Hoover came to the legislative session of 1932 in an atmosphere of crisis, ready for drastic measures. In his annual message to Congress, on December 8, 1931, Hoover first reviewed his own accomplishments of the past two years:

> Many undertakings have been organized and forwarded during the past year to meet the new and changing emergencies which have constantly confronted us . . . to cushion the violence of liquidation in industry and commerce, thus giving time for orderly readjustment of costs, inventories, and credits without panic and widespread bankruptcies.

Measures such as Federal and state and local public works, work sharing, maintaining wage rates ("a large majority have maintained wages at high levels" as before), curtailment of immigration, and the National Credit Corporation, Hoover declared, have served these purposes and fostered recovery. Now, Hoover urged more drastic action, and he presented the following program:

(1) Establish a Reconstruction Finance Corporation, which would use Treasury funds to lend to banks, industries, agricultural credit agencies, and local governments;

(2) Broaden the eligibility requirement for discounting at the Fed;

(3) Create a Home Loan Bank discount system to revive construction and employment measures which had been warmly endorsed by a National Housing Conference recently convened by Hoover for that

purpose;

(4) Expand government aid to Federal Land Banks;

(5) Set up a Public Works Administration to coordinate and expand Federal public works;

(6) Legalize Hoover's order restricting immigration;

(7) Do something to weaken "destructive competition" (i.e. competition) in natural resource use;

(8) Grant direct loans of $300 million to States for relief;

(9) Reform the bankruptcy laws (i.e., weaken protection for the creditor).

Hoover also displayed anxiety to "protect railroads from unregulated competition[18] and to bolster the bankrupt railroad lines. In addition, he called for sharing-the-work programs to save several millions from unemployment."[19]

As one can see from the passages above, many of the interventions associated with Roosevelt's New Deal were merely expansions on Hoover's policies. However, Roosevelt went much further in fundamentally changing the structure of America's economy. The New Deal represented a huge shift away from capitalism and towards a centrally-planned, socialist economy (combining elements of Soviet communism with Mussolini's fascism in Italy). This package of legislation and regulation is mistakenly credited with curing the Great Depression, when in fact it was the policies of FDR that caused it to last as long as it did. The prime reason is that all of his measures sought to preserve the artificial conditions created by Federal Reserve monetary inflation. When resources are misallocated, the solution is not to resist the market forces trying to reallocate them to productive use. This perpetuates the misallocation and the resulting economic crisis.

While the New Deal created a decade of misery in the 1930's, the worst thing about it was that it never really ended. The SEC, FCC, and most of the other regulatory agencies that stifle and distort our markets were created during this period. In addition, the National Labor Relations Act, which had a huge hand in the destruction of the American manufacturing sector, as well as Fannie Mae, which caused the mortgage crisis, were all created as part of FDR's New Deal. In addition, Social Security, one of the two entitlement juggernauts that threaten to bankrupt the government, was also created as part of Roosevelt's New Deal. The legacy of the FDR administration plagues our economy to this day, as most of its policies are still in effect, along with the Keynesian economic philosophy that inspired them.

In another striking parallel to the Great Depression, increased regulation is also being called for to cure the ill-effects of too much laissez faire capitalism. Remember that the Austrian school argues for little or no regulation on free markets at any time, especially during an adjustment period. They prescribe repealing existing regulations to help facilitate the adjustment.

It is useful to take a moment to define "regulation," as the term is used today. As opposed to laws, which are generally supposed to prohibit criminal behavior, regulations can generally be described more as more specific "rules" that stipulate how people must do certain things. In economic policy, regulations generally put conditions upon how certain exchanges of property are to take place. This should raise a red flag, because the non-aggression principle stipulates that the only limitation on property exchange is that it occurs with the mutual, voluntary consent of all parties. Nevertheless, commerce in America is regulated by a myriad of rules and governed by an alphabet soup of state and federal agencies.

As these regulations are increased, they begin to retard economic growth. This gives rise to calls for "deregulation." Deregulation, in the form of either opening up to the private sector markets for services previously provided by government, such as utilities, or reducing the amount of regulation on markets more highly regulated before, such as securities, are often represented as moving toward "more laissez faire capitalism." Often, however, deregulation consists of ceasing government intervention into one area of a particular economic market, while continuing to intervene in another.

This was true of the energy crisis in early 2000's California. Government deregulated some aspects of the market, but left price ceilings in place in parts of the supply chain, resulting in massive shortages and blackouts. Politicians represented this as a failure of capitalism, when in fact the blackouts were the result of government intervention: the price ceilings. The tragic irony is that, once capitalism is blamed, then more government - more of what caused the problem - is offered as the "solution."

This has been a recurring pattern. The government uses its coercive power to distort the market, under the pretense of achieving some laudable goal. By violating property rights and forcing people to make choices they would not otherwise make, systemic risks and conflicts are created that would not exist in a free market. To control the inevitable consequences, government then imposes a spider web of regulations. During periods of deregulation, some of the excessive controls are lifted, but the systemic risk is left in place. When the predictable disaster occurs, deregulation is blamed instead of the systemic problem itself. As insane as this might seem, we have repeated this pattern time and again over the past 100 years.

The mortgage crisis provides a perfect example of this. The government sponsored entities (GSE's) Fannie Mae and Freddie Mac created the crisis, with help from the Federal Reserve. Fannie Mae and Freddie Mac guaranteed mortgage loans with taxpayer money to people who would not have been able to obtain those loans in a free market. This is not capitalism, because the taxpayers did not consent to their money being put up as collateral for these loans.

In an attempt to prevent the predictable problems of financiers gambling with taxpayer money, regulations like the Glass-Steagall Act of 1933 were passed. A key component of Glass-Steagall prohibited traditional banks from acting as investment banks at the same time. This prevented the holders of mortgages guaranteed with taxpayer money from creating and selling securities based upon those mortgages, as well as other types of speculation. Those prohibitions were lifted with the passage of the Gramm-Leach-Bliley Act of 1999[20]. However, not only did the government not remove the systemic risk created by tax-backed loans, it actually encouraged Fannie Mae and Freddie Mac to take on even more and riskier loans than they had previously.[21] As a result, financiers were allowed to create complex derivatives and take inordinate risk, all with someone else's money. This was the cause of the huge housing bubble which triggered an economic meltdown of unprecedented proportion.

It is important to remember that the root cause of all of this was government intervention. By forcing taxpayers to guarantee loans, they allowed financiers to take risks they otherwise would not take. Without Fannie Mae and Freddie Mac to guarantee the loans, the defaulting mortgages wouldn't exist and the worthless mortgage-backed securities wouldn't have been sold. Yet, we choose to ignore the obvious and blame the free market instead. One is sometimes tempted to think we will find any excuse to give away our liberty.

So, regulations played a key part in creating the housing bubble. The idea that deregulation is to blame is obviously false. It is the underlying systemic imbalances created by government intervention that caused the crisis. While repealing Glass-Steagall may have aggravated it, it is clear that regulation has failed to shield us from the systemic problems government creates. Injustice cannot be solved by further injustice.

The past two hundred years have served as a great controlled experiment. During the 19th century, America's economy was arguably the freest, most capitalist in history. It was a century of unprecedented economic growth, culminating in an explosion of innovation that changed the world. In the fifty years between the end of the Civil War and 1915, mass production, telephones, the automobile, the airplane, the incandescent light, and countless other improvements transformed life from what it had been for thousands of years to what we now commonly call "the modern world." From 1812 to 1912, general price levels for average Americans were cut in half, doubling their real wages and raising their quality of life faster than in thousands of years of history combined.

The last century has been one of increasing government control over the economy, decreasing property rights, and socialism. While progress and innovation have continued, the trends of the 19th Century in terms of prosperity have largely reversed. In the mixed economy of the past century, prices have not only stopped decreasing, but have skyrocketed by over 2,200%. Economic growth has been able to curb the resulting decrease in real wages somewhat, but has not been enough to keep the living standards for most people from declining. The gap between rich and poor has widened. The percentage of people below the poverty line is increasing. The United States government is mired in debt that it cannot pay off.

While the results of the "great experiment" should seem as plain as day, most people seem to have accepted fallacious criticisms of capitalism, due to the misconceptions promoted about it, particularly during the 19th century. Detractors of capitalism have convinced Americans that the capitalist aspect of our mixed economy causes its problems, while the socialist aspect solves them or partially mitigates them.

The proof against this fallacy is everywhere. The freest economies of the 20th century were the most productive, including the United States, Hong Kong, and the freer economies of Europe. The most socialist economies were the least productive, including the communist regimes and the more socialist countries of Europe. Moreover, as countries have moved away from socialism and toward capitalism, they have become wealthier and their people have enjoyed an increasing standard of living. Russia, Viet Nam, and China have moved away from communism and are among the fastest growing economies in the world. The United States has moved closer to socialism and is suffering a very painful decline.

Most convincingly, we have seen these two economic ideologies each taken to their logical extremes. The United States practiced the most laissez faire capitalism that has ever been practiced in history during the 19th century. It resulted in an explosion of wealth, innovation, and increase in living standards unprecedented in human history.

In contrast, Russia and China practiced the purest socialism that has ever been practiced in human history. It resulted in mass starvation, the deaths of tens of millions of people, and eventual economic collapse.

There is only one hope for America. Americans must wake up to the obvious facts of economics and history and reject the propaganda they are fed by their government and media establishment. While a painful correction is inevitable at this point, America can still avoid complete collapse by recognizing freedom as the source of her former economic greatness, as well as the only means of restoring it. The other alternative is to continue on the present course, and hope for the best when the inevitable collapse occurs. History does not give great odds on a society in chaos choosing freedom. In fact, quite the contrary.

We have made only passing references to the role of monetary policy. The Austrian school points to monetary expansion as the ultimate source of economic crises, causing the initial speculative boom that precedes the crisis. They also argue that monetary expansion causes devaluation of the currency and a decrease in purchasing power for most members of society. The value of the U.S. dollar has been declining rapidly during the 21st century, although the imminent effects of that decline have not yet been felt. There is a very specific reason for this decline in value that we will examine in the next chapter.

For our purposes here, suffice it to say that inflation and its resulting destruction of the value of the currency have traditionally accompanied socialist or authoritarian societies, while sound currencies have accompanied capitalist or freer ones. From communist China and Russia to Nazi Germany to the more socialist mixed economies of Europe, the currencies of these societies have been more or less devalued to the extent that the nation in question has been more or less socialist. Even the Roman Empire finally collapsed in some part due to the debasement of its currency. The United States has been no exception to this rule. While it had the freest economy in history, it had a currency that constantly increased in value. As it has become more socialist in the 20th century, its currency has steadily declined.

It is not merely distortions caused by government intervention that debase the currency and cause prices to steadily rise. There is a more specific reason, directly related to the currency itself. "Inflation" is another word taken for granted by most people, but just as poorly understood. As we will see in the next chapter, there can be no liberty without sound money.

Chapter 6
The Money Monopoly

"That we are overdone with banking institutions, which have banished the precious metals, and substituted a more fluctuating and unsafe medium, that these have withdrawn capital from useful improvements and employments to nourish idlenesss, that the wars of the world have swollen our commerce beyond the wholesome limits of exchanging our own productions for our own wants, and that, for the emolument of a small proportion of our society, who prefer these demoralizing pursuits to labors useful to the whole, the peace of the whole is endangered, and all our present difficulties produced, are evils more easily to be deplored than remedied."

- Thomas Jefferson (1810)[1]

The most damaging government intervention into the marketplace is its manipulation of the value of money itself. It accomplishes this through the Federal Reserve System, the central bank of the United States. While many critics of the Federal Reserve correctly point out that it is a privately owned institution, it is important to remember the Fed was created by Congress. Its board of governors and its chairman are appointed by the president. It has a government-granted monopoly on the most important commodity in the world, the U.S. dollar. While some allege the Fed controls the government, instead of the other way around, the Fed certainly facilitates the government's agenda. Whatever the truth of their association, suffice it to say they have extremely common interests.

In order to understand the problems caused by the Federal Reserve System, one must have an understanding of fractional reserve banking. Preceding that, there is an even more fundamental question. What is money?

Like freedom, money is something most people take for granted until they are asked to define it. Then, money becomes a complete mystery. Considering all of the distortions it has suffered since the government got into the banking business, it is not surprising most people find it difficult to answer this simple question.

Money has two main purposes. It is a store of value and a medium of exchange. It is a practical way for people producing a wide variety of different goods and services to trade those goods and services with each other. It allows the grower of apples to trade with the manufacturer of automobiles without requiring the latter to accept 20,000 apples all at once.

Economists usually divide money into three categories. The first is commodity money. Commodity money is unique in that it has intrinsic value. While gold is often the example used, grain may be a better one to demonstrate this concept. At certain times in history, grain has been used as money. It is relatively uniform, easily divisible, somewhat imperishable, and scarce enough that it can function as money. If the automobile manufacturer trades his product for grain, he can store it for years without it spoiling. He can divide it into bushels, one pound sacks, cups, or even tablespoons, allowing him to buy goods and services of varying value. He can use it to trade for furniture for his house, or meat, or his electric service. If there are not sellers available to provide him something he wants in exchange for his grain, he can eat it. That is what is meant by "intrinsic value." It has a value inherent in itself. Gold and silver coins are also examples of commodity money.

Storing the necessary amount of grain to meet all of the needs for money in a modern society would be inconvenient, and carrying enough grain on your person to get through the day would be even more so. That is what gives rise to a second type of money, representative money. The U.S. dollar, when it was redeemable for a fixed amount of gold, was representative money. The defining characteristic of representative money is, while it has no intrinsic value of its own, it is directly redeemable for commodity money or a hard asset. This makes its value relatively stable, because you can always redeem it for grain, gold, or whatever hard asset the representative money is backed by.

The U.S. dollar today fits into a third category of money, fiat money. Fiat money neither has intrinsic value nor is it redeemable for a hard asset or commodity money. Its value is "bestowed upon it by fiat," and ultimately depends upon the confidence of those using it that it will be accepted in exchange for goods and services.

To facilitate an explanation of fractional reserve banking, it is helpful to clarify a term commonly used incorrectly. The word "inflation" is routinely used to describe rising prices and is often associated with the Federal Reserve's "Consumer Price Index" (CPI). This is not the true definition of inflation. Until very recently, the word "inflation" has always been used to describe an expansion of the money supply, not the resulting rise in prices. This is largely due to the way the Federal Reserve talks about inflation. They have a vested interest in associating inflation and all of its evils with the price increases themselves, rather than what causes them. The reason is simple. The Fed causes the price increases! While supply and demand influence price levels, it does not cause a uniform increase in demand or decrease in supply for most goods and services at the same time. Yet, Americans experience this steady increase in price levels for most goods and services over time. Like recessions, the government would have you believe this "just happens." It doesn't.

This subterfuge seems to have even been effective with the Merriam-Webster Dictionary. As late as its 1997 print edition Webster still defined inflation as "an increase in the volume of money and credit resulting in a continuing rise in the general price level." The present online Merriam-Webster dictionary defines inflation as "a continuing rise in the general price level usually attributed to an increase in the volume of money and credit relative to available goods and services." The people who work on publishing dictionaries take the integrity of words and their definitions very seriously, so accomplishing this complete reversal is no small accomplishment. Never underestimate the effectiveness of government spin!

It may seem complicated, but understanding money is really just common sense. All money, whether commodity, representative, or fiat, is subject to the same laws of supply and demand as anything other good. When the supply of money is increased, all other things being equal, then the prices of products that can be purchased with that money also increase. Inflation is properly defined as expansion of the supply of money, while rising prices are a result of inflation, not inflation itself.

It may come as a surprise, but steadily rising prices were not always a fact of life for Americans. That is a relatively recent phenomenon. The Federal Reserve publishes statistics on price levels that go back to 1800. Those statistics show that between 1800 and 1912, price levels increased in some years and decreased in others, but overall that there was a dramatic decrease in general price levels over that period of time. A basket of good that cost $100 in 1800 cost only $56.74 in 1912. From 1913 to 2008, that same basket of goods rose from $56.74 to $1,265.14.[2]. What was so special about 1913? That was the year the Federal Reserve System was created.

Decreasing prices are the natural result of economic growth. As companies become larger and more efficient, innovation increases productivity, lowering the cost of production. Sellers are able to produce more at a lower cost. This allows them to lower their price to buyers and still make a profit. Competition motivates them to do just that.

This is why new technologies are so much more expensive when they are first introduced then they are later. When the new technology first hits the market, the manufacturer has not yet maximized the efficiency of producing that technology. Each unit costs more to produce. As demand for the product increases, one might expect prices to go up. However, at the same time, the manufacturer is able to lower its production costs by buying its components in greater volume and therefore at lower unit costs, by utilizing more mass production methodology and automation, and by making improvements in the production process. The larger the manufacturer becomes, the more it benefits by what economists call "economies of scale." Decreases in production costs outpace increasing demand, resulting in the prices of new technologies decreasing over time. We have seen this most recently in the price histories of computers, cell phones, and other electronic technologies.

Thus, economic growth results in steadily lower prices over time, all things being equal. But all things are not equal. While America has become more and more productive over the past century, largely due to technological innovation, prices have generally increased, when economic law say they should have done exactly the opposite. The cause has been an enormous expansion of the money supply. Its resulting pressure on prices to rise has overcome the downward pressure on prices resulting from economic growth and innovation. Without this inflation, prices would likely be half of what they were 100 years ago, just prices in 1912 were half of what they were in 1800.

How does the money supply increase? It is constantly increased, albeit temporarily, by the practice of fractional reserve banking. Fractional reserve banking allows the bank to loan out most of the money on deposit while still keeping it simultaneously available to depositors. For example, when $100 is deposited in a savings account, the bank will loan out $90 of that money at interest. At the same time, your savings account will still show that you have $100 in the bank. Thus, $90 in new money has been created. This certainly provides a huge opportunity to the bank, which can make huge profits by charging interest on money that it creates out of thin air. It also allows the depositor to earn interest on a savings account, even if most of the money he deposited isn't really there. It can accelerate economic growth, by providing loans for business investment beyond the real savings of a particular economy.

However, as one might suspect, this is fraught with problems. One is the increase in prices we have already mentioned. The second is bank runs. Obviously, since the money lent to borrowers is also available for withdrawal by depositors, the bank does not have enough money to pay out if all depositors were to try to withdraw their deposits at the same time.

The central bank looks at withdrawal patterns on an ongoing basis to determine the "reserve ratio," which is the percentage of deposits banks are required to keep to honor the expected withdrawals by customers. Currently, the reserve ratio for most banks in the U.S. is 10%. That means that for all of the deposited money in the United States, banks can only honor withdrawals of 10% of those deposits at any given time.

This all works very well when the depositors generally have confidence that everyone else won't withdraw their money. When economic downturns or other factors undermine that confidence, depositors start withdrawing more of their money than usual. When confidence is completely lost, there is a "bank run," where depositors begin withdrawing all of their money at the same time. The bank only has the percentage of deposits they are required to keep on hand, so it very quickly runs out of money. This is known as a bank failure. The 2008 failure of the Indy Mac bank in California was one example.

While bank failures are catastrophic for depositors, they do generally keep the money supply stable, albeit by very painful means. Just as loaning your deposited money out created new money, the bank failure destroys money. A decrease in the money supply is known as "deflation."[3] If 90% of your deposit of $100 is available both to you and the borrower to whom it was lent, there is a total of $190 in existence related to your deposit. However, if the bank fails, that $90 of lent money is still in circulation, but your $100 is now gone. You have just helped stabilize the currency by losing what might be your life savings. The value of each dollar still in existence goes up as the total supply of dollars is decreased, just as the value of each dollar goes down as the total supply of dollars is increased.

Throughout history, fractional reserve banking and the inevitable bank failures that accompany it have motivated calls for a lender of last resort, or a central bank.[4] If you are going to allow fractional reserve banking, you must either resign yourself to bank failures and no "guaranteed" place to store and safeguard your savings, or that a central bank is necessary to create the money needed when banks cannot honor all of their withdrawal requests.

This represents a "trade-off" of sorts. When the central bank prevents bank failures, it is also preventing a shrinking of the money supply and a rise in the value of the currency. It also represents a decision to practice central planning of the monetary system, interest rates, and credit expansion, rather than leaving it to market forces and the invisible hand. As it does with the general economy, central planning in banking brings with it all of the foibles of socialism. Central banking is socialist, not capitalist.

Like other government interventions, central banking interrupts the natural cause and effect relationships in the marketplace. It perpetuates fractional reserve banking when it would otherwise fail. In order to artificially set interests rates, it purchases securities in large volume, causing an expansion of the money supply. If fractional reserve banking were a chemical reaction, the central bank would be the catalyst, accelerating the process with its infusions of "liquidity." That's why creation of the Fed in 1913 was so significant. Once money creation was no longer held in check by periodic bank failures or the restraint in credit expansion fear of bank runs might cultivate in banks, money supply began rapidly increasing, accompanied by the predictable increase in general price levels. This is the reason rising prices are a fact of life for Americans today.

Some argue inflation does no real harm because wages, the price of labor, also increase. However, history has shown wages are the last prices to increase. By contrast, the prices of commodities, like food, oil, steel, coal, and gold, increase the fastest. This drives up the costs food, energy and other necessities much faster than the increase in wages. Therefore, inflating the currency results in a general impoverishment of most people over time. That process has been ongoing since the Federal Reserve was created.

Many point to the 1950's as a period of great prosperity in the United States, even though the currency was still being inflated. This would seem at first to refute the theory.

There is a very simple explanation. The United States stayed out of World War II for the first three years it was being fought, but it served as a supplier of arms and other war materials for the Allies. As the outcome of the war was uncertain, the United States demanded payment for all of its arms sales in gold. Thus, by the end of the war, the United States had accumulated a huge percentage of the world's gold supply. This resulted in an artificial, one-time boost of the U.S. currency, which had otherwise been losing value steadily over the past 4 decades, despite the massive deflationary bank failures and decrease in money supply during the Great Depression.

This monetary phenomenon combined with the return of millions of U.S. servicemen to the workforce and huge cuts in government spending after the war. These three factors temporarily overcame the effects of government interventions, including monetary inflation, resulting in a brief period of relative prosperity. But the general trend of monetary inflation continued.

FDR had taken the U.S. dollar off of the gold standard domestically in the early 1930's, but the U.S. still allowed other countries to exchange U.S. dollars for gold. This policy combined with the relative strength of the U.S. currency due to the influx of gold from arms sales resulted in the Bretton Woods agreement, which made the U.S. dollar the reserve currency of the world. Now, most other countries pegged their fiat currencies to the dollar and began building up reserves of U.S. dollars to back them. This put upward pressure on the purchasing power of the U.S. dollar, resulting in an increase in real wages for Americans.

Had the Federal Reserve ceased inflating the supply of U.S. dollars, that trend would have continued. Instead, the Fed took advantage of the opportunity to inflate the currency at even greater rates. The Bretton Woods system broke down in 1971 when President Nixon "closed the gold window," telling the rest of the world that the U.S. dollar was no longer redeemable in gold. Since then, the U.S. dollar has been a completely fiat currency.

As previously mentioned, the Austrian school argues that the most egregious harm of inflation is its creation of what is commonly known as "the business cycle." This refers to the periodic booms and busts the American economy has experienced over the past 100 years. The government and the Fed always blame a myriad of villains, such as greedy Wall Street investors, the evil speculator, etc. In reality, the housing bubble, the tech bubble, and all of the previous economic bubbles, along with the inevitable recessions that followed them, have all been caused by the same thing: monetary inflation.

In addition to rising prices, inflation also causes malinvestment. Malinvestment is capitalists investing money into long term production projects that cannot be completed. These investment decisions are made based upon artificial conditions created by newly created money, instead of real savings. First, let us look at how it works without monetary inflation.

When voluntary saving increase, there is a corresponding drop in consumption. This has several consequences. The decreased demand puts downward pressure on consumer prices, resulting in generally lower interest rates. Inventories of consumer goods build up. These inventories sustain the economy as the long term projects are completed, making the productive structure capable of producing more than when the process started. The low interest rates make the projects profitable, considering the financing needed to complete them. When demand picks up again, the productive structure is generally able to supply more consumer goods, putting further downward pressure on prices to counteract the now increasing demand. The economy experiences an increase in the supply of consumer goods at the same or lower prices. The growth of the productive structure has also created new jobs. The overall result is an increase in wealth of the economy as a whole.[5]

However, when those investments in long term projects financed by inflation, an artificial boom occurs. No increase in voluntary savings has occurred, so there is no corresponding decrease in consumption. Thus, there is no drop in the prices of consumer goods and no inventories are built up to sustain the economy while the long term projects are completed. While the increase in the supply of money artificially lowers the interest rate, it only remains lower while the money supply continues to grow. Capitalists are investing in long term projects based upon artificially created conditions that make these projects appear profitable when they are not. They are also hiring people to fill newly created jobs that depend upon the long term projects being completed. Once the inflation ceases, interest rates naturally start to rise rapidly, due to consumer goods prices which have been rising all along. Ultimately, capitalists realize the long term projects are not going to be profitable and abandon them.

This is the "bust" part of the cycle, or the recession. The malinvestment is liquidated, and whatever capital goods that can be converted are applied to different projects. Some capital goods are too specific to the projects they were designed for, and have to be written off as a loss. The employees that were hired to fill newly created jobs must be let go when the projects are abandoned. Overall, there is a net loss of wealth after an artificial boom and bust period. At the end of the cycle, the productive structure is less able to produce as many goods, and must be rebuilt with voluntary savings or another artificial cycle. The employees must find jobs elsewhere.[6]

Sometimes monetary inflation causes entrepreneurs to misread not only long term interest rates and available savings, but the investments themselves. The cash rich environment leads some investors to start projects that wouldn't be profitable under any circumstances.

Normally, the scarcity of money and credit forces lenders to use high standards when deciding whether or not to make a loan. They will always make the investments they believe have the best combination of risk and return. The natural tendency for a lender is to limit risk, while seeking those investments with the highest and most certain return.

However, as the money supply is increased and there is still money available *after* the most optimal investments have been made, the remaining money gets invested in ventures that have more risk or less certain expectation of return or both. Loans are granted to people or companies that would not have received them without the additional "liquidity" available to lenders.

This was the case in the "tech bubble" of the 1990's, when many new internet-based companies were loaned huge amounts of capital to launch businesses that were not ultimately viable. When those projects were abandoned, all of that capital was lost.

When the money supply is inflated hundreds of billions or even trillions of dollars beyond real savings, you get what has come to be known as "a bubble." A bubble is a critical mass of malinvestment that causes whole sectors of the economy to become overvalued. Once it becomes obvious those investments are never going to yield a return, you get the bursting of the bubble, and a recession. During the recession, all of those malinvestments are liquidated, debts are paid down, and general contraction in the economy occurs.[7]

The most devastating effect of the bubble bursting, which is a recession, is the effect it has on employees. It is bad enough that a large group of businesses fail and their products and services are no longer available to consumers. There are many products we can do without and surviving companies to provide those we cannot. However, the majority of those newly created dollars were invested in hiring people. Once the bubble bursts and those companies go out of business or are forced to downsize, all of the new jobs created by the bubble are gone. Having been hired to support a now abandoned project, the employees now have to find new jobs. Recessions tend to result in fewer jobs immediately available than there are people who have been displaced.

Every major recession the United States has experienced since the creation of the Federal Reserve has been created by the Federal Reserve. While the Fed talks about recessions as if they just happen, and often holds itself up as the savior rushing in to repair the damage, nothing could be further from the truth. Each recession has been preceded by a period of monetary inflation by the Fed, which has set in motion the cycle just described.

The Great Depression was no different. The only reason it lasted so long was because there were presidents in office that firmly believed government intervention could solve the problem. Contrary to popular legend, FDR did not solve the Great Depression. He exacerbated and prolonged it. But its fundamental cause was an inflationary bubble caused by monetary inflation, the malinvestment that occurred because of it and the inevitable recession that followed. This is a constant cycle we still suffer today.

With all of the devastation monetary inflation wreaks on the economy, one would naturally wonder why it is allowed at all. The answer is simple. While most suffer from inflation, there are two groups of people who benefit.

The first group is Wall Street investors and the executives of large corporations. The newly created money is lent directly to them. The erosion of purchasing power takes time, so those who receive the money first get it before its value has decreased. They use it to invest in new companies or to expand existing ones. Some of this new investment is the malinvestment we previously discussed, but these are not the people that suffer. By the time the bubble bursts, they have acquired their wealth and insulated themselves from the losses. Let's look at a typical scenario.

The Federal Reserve forces the market interest rate down to encourage lending to business and stimulate economic growth. The Fed accomplishes this by purchasing U.S. Treasury bonds in open market operations, resulting in the banks it purchases them from having more cash on hand to lend. Since this money is actually created by the Fed, it represents an increase in the money supply, and is often referred to as "printing money." Since there is more cash on hand to be lent, the price of borrowing goes down. This is simply a function of supply and demand.

The banks that sold the Treasury bonds to the Fed now lend this newly created money to a new business with an unsound business plan. In other words, this business is not going to be profitable in the long term, as was the case with so many of the tech boom firms. However, as long as it has the ability to borrow money, the new business can grow, hiring new employees and producing more of its product. Some of the employees it hires are highly paid executives. These executives usually have "golden parachute" clauses in their contracts, meaning if they are fired, they are guaranteed a large sum of money, regardless of the company's performance.

Even though the business plan is not profitable in the long term, the revenues of the company can increase quite rapidly as the company expands its operation and produces and sells more product, even though its costs might be rising just as fast. The growth in sales encourages other investors to buy stock in the company, expecting the company will start turning profits once its infrastructure is built. The stock price of the company rises and the original investors are able to sell off their stock at a huge profit, often during an initial public offering (IPO).

They have now already made a huge return on their original investment, even though the company hasn't made a profit yet. Once they sell their stock, their risk is gone. In fact, stock prices typically rise enough during and right after the IPO that the original investors can make all they need by merely selling a portion of their stock, retaining the rest in case the company succeeds. If it does, the rest is gravy. If it fails, they are unharmed.

Now, let's move forward two or three years. It has become apparent the company's business model is not viable in the market, or the project simply cannot be completed because the savings to support it aren't out there. Either way, the company is not going to be profitable in the long term. Until now, its existence has relied upon its ability to obtain more credit. The banks are no longer willing to lend it more money. The company fails. Who wins and who loses?

The original investors already made a huge profit on their original investment, which was money created out of thin air and lent to them. They sold some or all of their stock in the IPO and can go on to the next investment. Even the initial loan is a liability of the company, which is now bankrupt and can't pay it back. The original investors win.

The company executives are going to lose their jobs, but they have two things going for them. First, they have been paid exorbitant salaries and bonuses for those three years, even though the company did not succeed. Three years at a salary of $500,000 per year is more money than the average family makes in thirty years. Some executives make even more. Second, their compensation packages usually include some amount of company stock, which most are smart enough to sell off after the IPO, when prices have spiked and before the future of the company is known.

Finally, there are the golden parachutes. The contracts executives negotiate usually include a payout if the executive is let go before the contract is up. Even if the executive is fired by the board because of poor performance, the company is often contractually obligated to pay the executive a huge sum of money. Generally, if there are no criminal charges related to the failure of the company, the executives win.

On the other hand, all of the employees are out of work and most of them do not receive any money when they are let go. Even if the company survives, a huge downsizing is likely, putting a large percentage of the employees out of work with no golden parachute to help break the fall. The employees lose.

Moreover, the company is still owned by someone. Someone bought the stock sold off by the original investors in the IPO. The stock continued to be traded while its price per share rose on hopes the company was a winner. By that time, large institutional investors likely bought into the company and now own a majority of its stock. Most of these institutional investors are pension funds and large investment houses that invest the money of average Americans. These investors realize the losses, either in their portfolios or retirement accounts. Small investors and average Americans lose.

The worst and most far-reaching effect of the cycle hurts almost everybody. By the time the economy reaches the bust, the effect on price levels in general from the monetary inflation has had time to work. General price levels have risen, while wages have not kept pace. Even when wages do eventually rise, they do not rise proportionally as much as other price levels. Wage earners become poorer in real terms. Those earning the lowest wages are hurt the most. Average Americans lose again. The poor are devastated.

What has just happened is a transfer of wealth, from average Americans to the privileged few that received newly printed money from the government. This has nothing to do with capitalism and everything to do with stealing. There was no voluntary exchange of property with those who paid for this debacle. Those who have saved U.S. dollars have just lost purchasing power without having made one bad investment. Their purchasing power was stolen by those who increased the money supply. What is most insidious is that this wealth was stolen silently, with very little opportunity for most of the victims to realize it or object.

There second beneficiary of inflation is the government itself. The government currently spends almost $4 trillion per year. While taxes are high, they are not high enough to underwrite this massive spending. It is never politically advantageous to go to the voters and tell them you are raising taxes, so politicians try to avoid it whenever they can. Since cutting spending means risking the support of those who benefit from it, they must find the money to make up the difference elsewhere. Where do they make up that difference? You guessed it. Inflation.

The national debt gets a decent amount of coverage by media outlets, but very few people realize how that debt is incurred. The process is simple but made to sound complicated by those who do not want you to catch on to the wealth transfer game.

The budget deficits are generally made up with government bonds. Assume the deficit this year is going to be $400 billion, which means the government is going to spend $400 billion more than it collects in taxes. It will therefore issue $400 billion in government bonds over the course of the year, which are promissory notes to pay the money back with interest. These are known as Treasury bills, or "T-bills."

Somebody has to be willing to buy those bonds. The government finds domestic and foreign investors to buy some of them, but there just aren't enough willing lenders in the world for the government to sell all of its bonds. However, there is one lender that will buy as much as the government wishes to sell: the Federal Reserve.

The remainder of the bonds is sold to the Federal Reserve, which is now owed that money back, plus interest. How can the Fed afford to buy so much debt? It prints the money, just as it does when attempting to stimulate the economy. While the Fed eventually returns most of its profits to the Treasury, by that time the damage has been done. The new money has been created and spent into the economy, resulting in all of the consequences of inflation previously discussed.

While our leaders would have us believe inflation is a fact of life and allowing banks to maintain a fractional reserve is necessary to modern civilization, there is an alternative, and it is not that we all carry around bushels full of grain. Jesus Huerta de Soto argues in *Money, Bank Credit, and Economic Cycles* that the answer is to require a 100% reserve ratio.[8] Combined with re-linking the currency to a hard asset, such as gold or silver, this would end the perennial cycle of credit expansion and recession. Obviously, it could not be accomplished in a day or a week, but certainly the reserve ratio could be raised in small increments. The Federal Reserve could shrink the money supply by raising the reserve requirement at each meeting. Or the Fed could be abolished and regulation of money returned to Congress. Congress alone is given the power to coin money and regulate its value.

Unfortunately, history shows that even elected legislatures are poor currency managers, often more prone to inflation than even central bankers. One of the reasons the framers of the Constitution gave the federal government the power to regulate commerce was the many inflationary schemes being perpetrated by the various states to escape debts. At that time, monetary inflation was openly recognized as a fraud to surreptitiously transfer wealth or renege on debt.

The solution most consistent with non-aggression is to leave regulation of the currency to the market, as it was in early America. The U.S. dollar was actually a copy of the Spanish dollar, which was the most popular of many currencies used at the time in what can only be described as a free market for money. The U.S. dollar emerged out of the market, rather than being forced upon it. Perhaps there is a lesson there for the future.

Like everything else, the answers to questions about monetary policy all revolve around freedom in the end. Socialism destroys productivity and siphons off savings, making inflation necessary as the only other means of investment in the productive structure. In order to be able to get back to a stable currency, we must rid society of the legal plunder that necessitates inflation in the first place. All socialist states have destroyed their currencies, because socialism is unsustainable. Freer market societies have enjoyed a currency whose value increased over time.

Chapter 7
The Non-Rights

"The moment the idea is admitted into society that property is not as sacred
as the laws of God, and that there is not a force of law and public justice to
protect it, anarchy and tyranny commence. If 'Thou shalt not covet' and
'Thou shalt not steal' were not commandments of Heaven, they must be
made inviolable precepts in every society before it can be civilized or made
free.""

– John Adams (1787)[1]

Politicians often employ the strategy of repeating a position so many times that people begin believing it. The most insidious use of this strategy has been in distorting the understanding of natural rights. While politicians routinely violate many of our true rights, they cause even more damage by promoting false ones. The result is not only a perversion of justice, but also disastrous economic consequences.

The entire justification for the mixed economy is based upon recognizing rights that don't really exist. For example, most Americans consider the cost of healthcare one of the most important issues facing society today. The solutions proposed by politicians couldn't be worse. They have always promoted a scheme where government provides or guarantees healthcare to everyone. Cost has always been an obstacle. In 2010, they solved that problem with the Patient Protection and Affordable Care Act. They made it illegal not to buy health insurance. Brilliant.

Popular support for government managed healthcare was achieved with the aforementioned strategy. Politicians repeated arguments for a false right so many times that people began to believe it to exist; that every American has a right to healthcare.

A right to healthcare is now universally accepted as "social justice," but is actually an endorsement of slavery. What is healthcare? It is the labor or product of the labor of healthcare providers, including doctors, nurses, technicians, hospitals, and pharmaceutical companies. No one can have a right to that.

If each individual has a right to the fruits of his or her own labor, then obviously other people cannot also have a right to them as well. Two parties cannot have a right to the same goods. That's why one cannot claim a right to healthcare anymore than one can claim a right to a stereo or a swimming pool. It may be our wish that healthcare is available and affordable to everyone. There is nothing wrong with that. However, we cannot grant people a right to someone else's labor. That is slavery, by definition.

The statement "everyone has a right to healthcare" really means that everyone has a right to go into his doctor's office and demand to be evaluated and treated for free, under the threat of government force if the doctor doesn't comply. While this may seem bizarre, what we do in actuality is not any less so. Instead of directly enslaving the doctor, we instead have government forcibly extort the doctor's fee from taxpayers, resulting in a third party slavery.

Healthcare should be treated like any other exchange of property. Buyer and seller make an exchange by mutual, voluntary consent. This is the only way healthcare can be delivered without violating the non-aggression principle. It is the only way it can be delivered by and to free people.

Some argue healthcare must be made available to all because "it is a necessity." Let us assume it is. What are the other basic necessities of life and how are they provided? Food, clothing, and shelter are all provided in our society by voluntary exchange in a free market. In other words, they are all purchased by buyers from sellers. Of those three, government is less involved in food and clothing than it is in shelter (housing), and it is no coincidence food and clothing are generally more affordable. While the poorest members of society would like better food and nicer clothing, almost no one goes without. There is no outcry for the government to take over the food or clothing industry, and obviously both are more vital necessities than healthcare. The argument that government should provide healthcare because it is a necessity is without merit.

It is also said healthcare is too expensive for the poor and elderly to afford, and so those groups would go without it if it were not provided by the government. This is based upon fallacies about how the market works. Healthcare has only become so expensive because government provides it to so many people. As we have seen, the normal pattern in a free market is for prices to fall over time, not rise. Price is determined by the intersection of supply and demand. As an industry becomes more efficient, and the companies that provide a good or service become larger and can benefit from economies of scale, the cost of production of that good or service goes down. Competition ensures that sellers will offer their products at the lowest price possible in an effort to win business from their competitors. There is nothing magical about the healthcare industry that would make its economics any different. Without government interference, the price of healthcare would decrease over time, until it was readily available and affordable to even the poorest in society.

Government intervention into the healthcare market has prevented this natural phenomenon. Government artificially increases demand, which in turn pushes up price. To understand this, one must be using the correct definition of demand. As Bernstein points out, demand is not merely the desire to purchase a certain product, but also the ability to purchase it. In his own words, "a market requires people who possess purchasing power."[2] If demand were merely the desire to purchase a product, there would be unlimited demand for every product, and running a successful business would not be much of a challenge!

By making healthcare an entitlement and using the taxing power to fund it, there is literally no limit to the purchasing power of those receiving government healthcare benefits. For most products, the price can only go so high before people must make the decision to do without them. Not so with government-provided healthcare. The recipients are entitled the product. Therefore, it *must* be purchased for them, no matter how high the cost. The market forces that would lower the cost are eliminated and the price constantly rises. This is the unintended but inevitable consequence of government providing healthcare.

If government subsidization were removed from the healthcare industry, the artificial demand would disappear, resulting in a dramatic reduction in price. It is not as if without government there would be no healthcare industry. It existed throughout our history before government began subsidizing it. It would continue to exist if government ceased to subsidize it. There would still be doctors that need patients in order to make a living. They would have to find a way to provide their services at a price patients could afford. Price would be determined by the intersection of supply and *real* demand, rather than the artificial demand created by government.

This does not necessarily mean doctors would have to accept lower compensation. Other professionals, such as attorneys, accountants, and insurance agents all offer their services to clients without subsidization by government. They are some of the most highly paid professionals in society. They have found a way to deliver those services efficiently at a price their clients can afford and still enjoy high earnings.

Neither would quality of care be compromised if the industry were subjected to the free market. On the contrary, we have seen that the profit motive and competition actually increases quality while lowering price. It is widely believed that quality of care has declined in recent years due to cost cutting associated with managed care, but managed care came along at a time when government was already deeply entrenched in the healthcare industry. Healthcare hasn't been a free marketplace for decades. If it were allowed to be, we would see the natural increase in quality and availability and decrease in price we have seen in every other industry upon which free market forces were allowed to act.

Therefore, a major step in putting Americans back on the road to freedom would be to formulate a plan to phase out the government healthcare programs. Even if done gradually, this would involve some hardship in the short term. It will take time for the healthcare industry to adjust to the market and for providers to devise ways to deliver quality service at much lower prices, although industries can generally realign themselves in a matter of years, not decades. That the healthcare industry is made up of some of the brightest individuals in society bodes well for a speedier realignment than perhaps in other industries.

However we decide to do it, it must be done. There is no alternative. Medicare alone has tens of trillions in unfunded liabilities. The next economic disaster could accelerate complete insolvency of the program, which will occur at some point in the future anyway. We can either choose to phase out the programs as smoothly as possible or face that day in the perhaps not so distant future when the checks begin bouncing and there is no care for anyone.

Without repeating each step of the analysis, the same conclusions hold wherever government intervenes into the marketplace. The evidence is literally hiding in plain sight. Government is most heavily involved in healthcare, housing, and education and these three represent the costliest goods and services in society. Moreover, as government involvement in providing them has increased, the disproportionate costs of these products increased. They will continue to increase in cost until all resources are consumed trying to provide them.[3]

One need only look to the recent "housing bubble" for proof of government's distortion of the housing market. While government officials consistently try to shift the blame to "speculators" or "greedy, predatory lenders," the root cause was just more artificial demand created by the government. The Federal Reserve provided the new money and Fannie Mae and Freddie Mac, two government sponsored entities, made it possible for millions of people to get home loans they would not have been able to get in a free market. While the desire to see people with lower incomes own their own homes is laudable, intervention into the market caused people to get homes that they could not afford. This artificial demand resulted in the skyrocketing prices of housing and the inevitable cascade of foreclosures.

Government similarly intervenes with its "Section 8" program. Again, the intention is admirable. However, the same results occur when government intervenes in the rental market as occur in real estate or healthcare. Artificial demand is created, which inflates the price. This makes it profitable for absentee landlords to own these properties when it might not be profitable otherwise, thus decreasing the percentage of homes owned by people that live in the neighborhood. An absentee landlord has little incentive to spend money on upkeep of the property beyond the minimum requirements, which is why poorer neighborhoods often become so dilapidated. The intervention not only drives up prices, making rent harder for the poor to afford, but also contributes to poorer living conditions for the people it intends to help. If government were to cease subsidizing the rental industry, prices would immediately fall, making most of those rents affordable even to the poor families that presently require government assistance to rent them.

If there is any public institution that even the most liberty-minded person is predisposed to defend, it is public education. Although it is hard to make this leap, education, like healthcare, is just the labor of those who provide it. Teachers, education administrators, and others in the education industry create the product we call "education." While everyone has a right to offer to purchase education, no one has a right to be *provided with* education. Like any other product, the most morally justified and effective way for it to be distributed is by voluntary exchange in a free market.

Government intervention in the form of student loans yields the same results in education as it does in any other industry. By artificially creating demand underwritten by taxpayers, government has caused tuition to skyrocket since it started "helping students go to college."

For anyone whose parents worked their way through school, this should be obvious. Before the prevalence of student loans, it was possible to earn enough money with summer and part-time jobs to pay college tuition, sometimes assisted by discounts or partial scholarships offered by the colleges. Summer and part-time jobs available to inexperienced college students didn't pay executive salaries back then. College was just a lot cheaper in real terms. To suggest that a job at McDonalds or a department store could provide enough money to pay for a college education today is obviously laughable. Yet, this is exactly how millions of Americans did it before government got involved.

When government tries to provide things to citizens, it makes them less available and more expensive. It also erodes the quality of the goods or services it attempts to provide. We now have a full century of increasing government involvement in the marketplace to evaluate. The results are undeniable. Central government planning of the economy has failed.

However, the most compelling argument to cease government involvement in healthcare, housing, education, and other segments of the marketplace is not a utilitarian argument. It is a moral one. In order to run any of these programs, government must violate the most basic rights of its citizens. It must forcibly seize the property of one individual in order to provide it to another.

These moral and practical arguments hold equally for the rest of the government entitlements, including social security and traditional welfare. Whatever the good intentions of those who founded the programs, they represent the armed theft of property from one individual for the purpose of redistribution to another. Ultimately, they do not even help the recipients significantly, due to the limitations of even forcibly collected revenues. Just ask a welfare recipient how they are enjoying life on the pittance they collect. Everyone, including its strongest proponents, agrees public education is a spectacular failure. We must finally realize that poor results in terms of quality, availability, and price are not the result of poor administration, but an inherent problem in any government-provided service. When individuals trade voluntarily, they strive to offer the best they possibly can. When they are forced to provide something under the threat of violence, all of those incentives are eliminated.

Social Security is also unsustainable, for all of the same reasons. With an understanding basic economics, it should seem like complete lunacy to expect government not only to provide specific goods or services, like healthcare, but to actually pick up all of our living expense after we reach a certain age. Yet, this is exactly what Social Security purports to be able to do![4] Like Medicare, it will eventually go bankrupt, and again that day is only distant if the U.S. economy continues to grow. Current economic trends could move up Social Security's insolvency date dramatically.

The bizarre results of attempting to secure these non-rights further demonstrate the failure of the mixed economy. The market does not tolerate compromise. You cannot "force people a little." Even the United States, which attempted to mix its economy with the most free market capitalism, has eventually run into the same problems that the communist countries did. The other mixed economies are even less sustainable, as the imminent worldwide economic crisis will reveal. Prosperity will only be restored by returning to laissez faire capitalism, the economics of freedom. While there are challenges to doing so and a painful transition to make, it is really the only viable solution.

Chapter 8
The Slavery Tax

"A capitation is more natural to slavery; a duty on merchandise is more natural to liberty, by reason it has not so direct a relation to the person."

Montesquieu (1748)[1]

The non-aggression principle poses a dilemma regarding paying for government. Requiring individuals to purchase protection of their property from an organization created by others is incompatible with the principle. True consent can only be given individually. Majority votes are simply the best compromise with individual consent a government can offer. Even a very limited government compromises the non-aggression principle by existing at all. That it must force its constituents to support it financially compromises the principle further.

The American founders adopted Locke's justification for the existence of government. He said that in the state of nature man is in a state of perfect liberty and not under the jurisdiction of any government. With no government, there are no taxes. However, Locke says there are disadvantages to this state.

"First, There wants an established, settled, known law, received and allowed by common consent to be the standard of right and wrong, and the common measure to decide all controversies between them: for though the law of nature be plain and intelligible to all rational creatures; yet men being biased by their interest, as well as ignorant for want of study of it, are not apt to allow of it as a law binding to them in the application of it to their particular cases.

Secondly, In the state of nature there wants a known and indifferent judge, with authority to determine all differences according to the established law: for everyone in that state being both judge and executioner of the law of nature, men being partial to themselves, passion and revenge is very apt to carry them too far, and with too much heat, in their own cases; as well as negligence, and unconcernedness, to make them too remiss in other men's.

Thirdly, In the state of nature there often wants power to back and support the sentence when right, and to give it due execution, They who by any injustice offended, will seldom fail, where they are able, by force to make good their injustice; such resistance many times makes the punishment dangerous, and frequently destructive, to those who attempt it."[2]

Thus, while there is the general law of nature, the non-aggression principle, there are no specific laws that apply the principle to specific circumstances. Neither are there judges to act as dispassionate arbitrators, meaning self-interest will make it unlikely most disputes can be resolved. Most importantly, there is no power to enforce the law of nature, other than the individual's ability to enforce it him or herself. Thus, the state of nature results in "might makes right," regardless of the justice of the stronger party's position.

For these reasons, Locke says men rarely remain in a state of nature for long, and "take sanctuary under the established laws of government, and therein seek the preservation of their property." [3]

For Locke and the founders, government was necessary for the law of nature to be practically enforced. Without government, although each individual has a right to life, liberty, and property, there is no guarantee those rights will be respected by everyone. Thus, reason dictates that in order to preserve his natural rights, in order to be able to live by the non-aggression principle, man needs government to protect him. It is by this reasoning the founders were able to reconcile themselves that government must exist and that even free individuals had a responsibility to pay taxes.

However, there was still the question of how to assess the tax.

Working within Locke's philosophical framework, the founders' ideas about taxation were exactly the opposite of our ideas about it today. Rather than a "fair share" citizens owed to society, they viewed taxation as a necessary evil, which should be as limited and as non-compulsory as possible. Since the purpose of government was limited to protecting life, liberty, and property, the founders intended that enough money would be collected for that purpose and not a penny more. In the Constitution, they insisted taxation should be indirect. Until the passage of the 16th Amendment in 1913, the majority of federal government taxes were tariffs, or taxes on imports. Tariffs achieved the objective of making taxes as indirect and non-compulsory as possible. As Madison said,

"...a national revenue must be obtained; but the system must be such a one, that, while it secures the object of revenue it shall not be oppressive to our constituents."[4]

In his second inaugural address, Thomas Jefferson celebrated that all taxation other than tariffs had been eliminated.

"The suppression of unnecessary offices, of useless establishments and expenses, enabled us to discontinue our internal taxes. These covering our land with officers, and opening our doors to their intrusions, had already begun that process of domiciliary vexation which, once entered, is scarcely to be restrained from reaching successively every article of produce and property...The remaining revenue on the consumption of foreign articles, is paid cheerfully by those who can afford to add foreign luxuries to domestic comforts, being collected on our seaboards and frontiers only, and incorporated with the transactions of our mercantile citizens, it may be the pleasure and pride of an American to ask, what farmer, what mechanic, what laborer, ever sees a tax-gatherer of the United States?"[5]

While conservative politicians today argue for tax cuts, usually as stimulus for the economy, it is quite a different thing to hear a U.S. president rejoice that internal taxation had been eliminated completely. Yet, this is what had happened by the end of Jefferson's first term.

Recognizing the ultimate authority of the people over those collecting the taxes, Jefferson had this to say to the British Parliament in 1775,

"That this privilege of giving or withholding our monies is an important barrier against the undue exertion of prerogative, which if left altogether without control may be exercised to our great oppression; and all history shews how efficacious is its intercession for redress of grievances and reestablishment of rights, and how improvident it would be to part with so powerful a mediator."[6]

Jefferson asserted a right of the people to withhold their tax money from government if the government were to misuse it to violate the rights of the people.

The assumption underlying all of these positions is that only the amount of money absolutely necessary to protect the life, liberty, and property of the people should be collected. The people give up only that small portion of their property necessary to protect the rest. They pay the government for a service that has a finite cost and the government has no legitimate claim on anything beyond that cost. Moreover, it is an expectation of government to provide this service as efficiently, at as low a cost to the people as possible. The people even retain the right to withhold their tax money if they are not satisfied with how it is being spent. Most importantly, the total amount the government needs to collect in taxes to support such a limited scope is very, very small.

The underlying assumption of an income tax is exactly the opposite. By requiring a percentage of each person's income, there is no limit to what is due to the government. If the tax is twenty-eight percent, then government is entitled to $28,000 on $100,000 in taxable income, and $280,000 if income increases to $1 million. The more productive and prosperous society becomes, the bigger and more oppressive its government. Both philosophically and from a utilitarian standpoint, an income tax is the most hostile to liberty.

We have established that one of the most vital of the inalienable rights is the right of each individual to the fruits of his labor. Jefferson called it "the first rule of association." Samuel Adams called it "the first law of nature." The right to keep the product of one's labor is necessary to sustain one's existence. When government makes an unlimited claim on a percentage of the individual's labor, it is really claiming partial ownership of the individual himself. This is tantamount to slavery.

While the income tax does not claim all of the individual's labor, as the slave master does, what is left to the individual is no longer a right, but a privilege. If the government decides to raise the tax, the individual must pay, regardless of his consent. For all intents and purposes, his property rights are gone.

It is true that any taxation is a tax on the individual's labor, since all property has its origins in labor. However, there is a substantive difference between a tax on consumption, which the individual can limit or avoid if he wishes, and one on every penny he earns. While tariffs may or may not be as attractive a solution in today's global economy, it is clear that an indirect tax is infinitely more consistent with liberty. Most importantly, only the amount necessary to protect the life, liberty, and property of the citizens should be collected, no matter what the method of assessment.

Americans might be quite surprised at how small that expense would be. Without the trillions in annual expenditures on entitlement programs and Defense (most of which is spent defending other countries), no income tax would be necessary. Even outside of these two large categories, most other federal government spending is for activities other than protection of life, liberty and property.

Jefferson also alluded to a further evil of taxation, which is the necessity of ensuring compliance. Even the consumption taxes imposed in Jefferson's time necessitated what he considered too much intrusion into the lives of the people. Contrast that with our situation today. American citizens are required to keep an accurate accounting of every penny they make and report it to the government. This violates the principle that government power must be limited to negative power, which prohibits actions that harm others but doesn't force people to do anything.

Not only does the income tax require Americans to report to the IRS, it assumes the taxpayer is guilty of non-compliance until he proves his innocence. Furthermore, by setting the tax high and then "allowing" the taxpayer to take deductions for business expenses, charitable contributions, and certain necessities, the taxpayer is reduced to begging the IRS to be allowed to keep his own money. This is not consistent with a relationship between sovereign individual and servant government. It is exactly the opposite. By taxing income, the government makes liberty virtually impossible.

Lastly, the income tax has a destructive effect on the economy. By removing trillions of dollars, it destroys capital that could otherwise be used to invest in production. Government doesn't produce anything. That capital is simply consumed. Another $325 billion per year is spent by firms and individuals just trying to comply with the labyrinthine tax code, wasting even more capital.[7]

Some believe a functional government and a stable society would be impossible without taxing incomes. It is not impossible. We did it right here in America for over one hundred and thirty years, while becoming the wealthiest, most powerful nation in human history. The Industrial Revolution occurred in an America without an income tax. As we have seen over and over again, respecting individual rights produces tangible, positive results. Violating those rights consistently results in disaster. Our method of taxation is no different. A key step in returning prosperity and economic growth is to restore to everyone the most important civil liberty of all: the right to the fruits of one's labor. We must abolish the insidious tax on income.

Chapter 9
The Socialism Bubble

"He who is permitted by law to have no property of his own, can with difficulty conceive that property is founded in anything but force."

– Thomas Jefferson (1788)[1]

In 2008, the federal government bailed out the financial institutions that were facing bankruptcy in a massive intervention. Even most of those opposed to the bailout bill did not understand what was happening. One faction argued the bailout wasn't necessary to prevent the stock market crash (it crashed anyway). The government argued that a credit squeeze would result in unemployment, while the other side argued unemployment would not necessarily have resulted if the bailout had not passed. Another group blamed the crisis on too little regulation.

All of these positions were wrong. As we now know, there has been a painful adjustment in the stock market. Massive unemployment followed, regardless of any intervention by the government. The only question is how long it will last. That is reality when any bubble deflates.

The most unfortunate result was that some Americans supported government intervention *because* there were market losses and high unemployment. Their initial instinct to oppose the bailout of the financial institutions was correct. As the Austrian school of economics argues, the losses those companies suffered due to massive malinvestment were real. That eventually had to be reflected in the value of their stocks.

It is similarly unfortunate that many Americans believe more regulation can prevent this from happening again. More regulation will not prevent a problem in large part caused by too much regulation. Contrary to government propaganda about the crisis, we are in the midst of an economic correction that has been a century in the making and for which government is entirely responsible.

We have heard about the "tech bubble," the "housing bubble," and even the "dollar bubble." All of these are real. The dollar bubble is about to burst, with global consequences. But even that is not the biggest bubble. The biggest is what I call "the socialism bubble."

As we saw in an earlier chapter, the term "bubble" is used in economics to describe a large misallocation of resources (malinvestment). The central bank artificially infuses money and credit into the economy, that money flows toward projects that appear to be profitable under the artificially created conditions, but aren't, and those projects ultimately fail, causing the bursting of the bubble. The worst part of a bubble bursting is that the greatest misallocation of resources has been of human resources. Those people now have to find new jobs. They have to be reemployed elsewhere, in profitable ventures, as do the capital goods that were misallocated to the projects. That is why unemployment accompanies recessions.

The socialism bubble is also a misallocation of resources. It has just taken longer to form and is much larger in scope. The principles behind it are the same. It has been caused by government intervening into the economy to create artificial conditions that misallocate resources. Under these artificial conditions, the entire economy appears to be profitable, but isn't. When the inevitable burst occurs, all of the misallocated resources, including human resources, become unemployed. We are about to experience a massive correction when this bubble bursts.

The socialism bubble started at the turn of the last century. The United States of the 19th century had the closest system to laissez faire capitalism ever achieved in history, arguably followed next by Great Britain. The defining principle of laissez faire capitalism is voluntary exchange. With everyone acting in their rational self-interest, the minds of all participants are leveraged by the system to consistently produce optimal results.

In the laissez faire marketplace of the 19th century, wages rose modestly. Economic ignorance caused social reformers to condemn the free market for this.[2] They ignored that the general price level fell, making workers much richer in real terms. They attempted to improve on the results that laissez faire capitalism had produced with government policy.

There is only one alternative to voluntary exchange: involuntary exchange. Government economic policies force economic agents to make choices they otherwise would not make. No matter how one tries to euphemize socialism, that is what it is. By attacking voluntary exchange, socialism attacks the mechanism that creates wealth.

Rising costs of production are one result. Government cannot force an automobile company to pay their employees more, provide them healthcare or pensions, follow a spider web of regulations of its operations, and expect the company's cost of making automobiles not to rise. As the cost of production rises, the company must find a way to keep costs below the market retail price. They might decide to manufacture SUV's, which have larger margins, even though a spike in gasoline prices could put them out of business (see General Motors).

The truth is that none of the American auto manufacturers are able to produce an automobile that is competitive in the market. The government has a host of villains to blame for this, but look at the balance sheets of the Big Three. It is abundantly clear why they are not viable. Concessions to labor unions (mandated by government) have made it too expensive for them to operate.

Some argue that "unregulated capitalism" caused American manufacturing jobs to migrate overseas, where manufacturing labor was cheaper. This fallacy refutes itself. If "market forces" truly were in play, how did U.S. labor costs get so high? Did "greedy capitalists" simply abandon their profit ambitions and decide to pay their employees more than they could afford to? Why didn't capitalist greed prevent these concessions?

Of course, everyone knows the answers to these questions, but want to pretend they don't. The reason manufacturers, especially the automakers, continually promised labor unions more than they could afford to pay was because the government forced them to do so. Under the euphemism "collective bargaining," the government made it illegal for a manufacturer to refuse a demand from a union. An illusion of choice was sustained by merely requiring the employer "make a reasonable counter-offer," but the courts were there to see that "reasonable" meant if the union asked for the moon and the stars, the employer would have to at least agree to a few planets. In the end, the employer could not choose freely what to pay their employees or what benefits to offer. Without free choices, market forces are eliminated.

As with so many other systemic economic problems, the entire union concession/cost escalation dynamic goes back to the New Deal, specifically the National Labor Relations Act of 1935. It was this fundamental departure from capitalism that sowed the seeds of the destruction of American manufacturing. Americans actually observe this government coercion and call it "unregulated capitalism" and the series of concessions made by manufacturers at gunpoint as "market forces." We are truly through the looking glass where a bull is stumbling through the china shop and the storekeeper is reprimanding the broken glass.

While it might at first seem unfair to blame sixty year old legislation for the failure of a company in 2008, one must consider the dominance that America enjoyed in manufacturing to begin with. At one time, American manufacturers flooded the world with high-quality, low-cost goods, while still paying wages many times higher than their competitors overseas. There was no sector where America was more dominant than automobile manufacturing, an industry the country practically invented. It would not be brought to bankruptcy overnight. Year after year, decade after decade, the companies grew a little less profitable as costs rose. It was not until decades later that those costs rose beyond the point where the companies could remain competitive.

The length of time it took for the disease to run its course does not change the nature of the virus that caused it.

The same reasoning applies to other sectors of the economy. The collapse we are experiencing is the result of an economy rendered profoundly unproductive by systemic problems that all relate to government intervention.

These are the real reasons for America's loss of manufacturing infrastructure. It is simply not economically viable to manufacture anything in the United States anymore. This is not a natural result of free markets. Wages and other costs of production fell under the laissez faire system. Falling prices are a natural result of economic growth and innovation. The artificial conditions created by government intervention have made it expensive to make things in America.

Rising production costs are not the only pressures on the American economy. Entitlement programs currently consume 12% of GDP. Keynesians say this is not harmful because the recipients spend that money and increase demand. Hopefully, the coming calamity will discredit this economic school of charlatans once and for all. Wealth is created by production, not consumption. Redistribution destroys voluntary savings and ultimately capital. It also eliminates other conditions that accompany voluntary savings and facilitate natural expansion of the productive structure.

Increasing socialism has put artificial, negative pressures on the American economy for almost a century. Those pressures have accumulated to make America profoundly less productive. Like the communist countries, we have lived in a dream world where government could use brute force to change economic reality. We have pretended businesses can spend more than they take in and continue to survive. For a time, the free market aspects of America's "mixed economy" overcame these negative pressures. That time has passed. Economic reality is about to assert itself in devastating fashion.

For at least two decades now, Americas have been producing far less than they consume. All things being equal, this would not have lasted long. All things are not equal. The United States has a central bank and the privilege of printing the world's reserve currency. This is why the socialism bubble has become so enormous.

Instead decreased consumption and rising unemployment[3] as manufacturing migrated overseas, America went right on consuming. Employees found new jobs in the "service economy." With the Federal Reserve providing an unlimited supply of fiat currency and the ability to export that inflation overseas by importing foreign goods in exchange for U.S. dollars, America has been able to maintain the same standard of living. As long as foreigners accepts U.S. dollars, the dream world can persist. The bubble continues to inflate.

Ominously, a large percentage of the American labor force is now misallocated by this bubble. There are tens of millions of American workers employed in ventures that will cease to exist once it bursts. We have seen the beginning with failures of large retailers and restaurant chains. That is only the tip of the iceberg. Unlike previous recessions, there are no manufacturing jobs for these displaced workers to redeploy to. The productive structure must be rebuilt. That doesn't happen overnight.

Americans must realize further equity market losses[3] and mass unemployment are inevitable. The only question now is how long those undesirable conditions will last. There is no solution, government or otherwise, that will allow us to avoid this correction. If the government ceases intervention, the period of adjustment will be shorter. If the government continues to intervene, the adjustment period will be longer, with continued new malinvestment even as liquidation of current malinvestment occurs. Contrary to what we are taught in public schools, government intervention identical to what we are seeing now was the cause of the Great Depression, not its solution.

The only path to a true recovery is a return to the laissez faire capitalism that made America prosperous in the first place. This would include eliminating unnecessary regulation, abolishing the central bank and restoring sound money, eliminating minimum wages and other artificial price controls, capping and eventually phasing out the entitlement programs, eliminating other massive government spending on military bases overseas and unnecessary war, and restoring contract law and protection of property rights. In other words, freedom.

Chapter 10
The War On…

"Those who would give up Essential Liberty to purchase a little Temporary Safety deserve neither Liberty nor Safety"

– attributed to Benjamin Franklin[1]

People make decisions differently in an emergency. Whatever might be important to them under normal circumstances, the sole concern in an emergency is safety from the immediate threat. During a flood, the sole concern is to keep from drowning. In a fire, the sole concern is to keep from being burned alive. In war, to defeat the enemy before he kills or enslaves you.

Individuals in the emergency are willing to take direct orders from policeman, fireman, or soldiers in order to avoid danger and flee to safety. No one escaping a burning building stops to question the authority of the fireman who orders him to run this way or that. Trust is placed in authority in exchange for safety. Once the danger has passed, the individual reclaims his independence. This natural shift in perspective during an emergency helps those untrained to deal with the emergency survive.

In times of war, this state of emergency lasts much longer. It is assumed the population faces the very real danger that a foreign army may invade their country, occupy their cities, and abolish their liberty.[2] The state of emergency that accompanies any real war often necessitates the sacrifice of personal freedoms in exchange for security, especially if the enemy is close at hand and has a reasonable chance of victory.

While there is room for debate as to whether the government is justified in temporarily infringing upon certain rights during a dire wartime emergency, there is no justification for such infringement over a non-emergent social problem. This is precisely what has happened as a result of government's various domestic "wars." These might be merely public relations gimmicks to convince the public that the government is really, really serious, but they carry far more ominous consequences.

Once government's mandate to enforce the law becomes a war, all of the conditions that accompany a state of emergency come with it. No longer are individual rights or personal liberty a consideration. They must be sacrificed to avoid the immediate threat. Worse, unlike a military war, which has a beginning and an end, the government's War on Poverty, War on Drugs, and more general War on Crime have no end. They are wars that can never be won, and so the state of emergency, along with its subjugation of individual rights, persists indefinitely.

Today, few would argue the War on Drugs has not been a failure. Despite incarcerating millions of Americans and spending hundreds of billions of dollars, drug use has never been higher. Time after time, we see members of the police force sent out to enforce laws against this non-crime are drawn into the drug trade themselves, due to the enormous profits available in any black market. As they did during alcohol prohibition, the huge profits have also promoted the growth of a myriad of criminal organizations.

Each year, more personal liberty is lost because the solution to last year's failure to "win the war" is to try to further eliminate the *opportunity* to commit the crime this year. To detect the laundering of drug money, everyone's financial transactions must be watched for suspicious activity. To prevent drugs from being transported by air, inspections of everyone's belongings must be conducted at airports. There are even devices that use x-rays to see into people's houses; used if there is any suspicion they may be growing marijuana. As time goes on and the "War on Drugs" continues to fail, more individual rights will be lost until everyone is presumed guilty until proven innocent; all to "protect us" against activity that harms no one but the actor.

The same is true of the more general War on Crime. That is not to say crime shouldn't be punished. Those who commit aggression against life, liberty or property should be arrested and prosecuted. Crime and punishment is part of everyday life. By prosecuting and punishing *real* crime, individual rights are defended.

However, once this is transformed into a war, all sense of normalcy changes. The rights of the people become secondary to winning the war. A state of emergency exists and only ending the emergency can bring normalcy back to society and the respect for individual rights. But the emergency can't end because there will always be crime. No matter how many are arrested, no matter how many rights are lost, no matter how draconian the measures taken to prevent crime, it will persist. Thus, the state of emergency will never end and the rights suspended to deal with it will never be restored. This has been the result of every "war" the government has fought against social issues.

The War on Poverty resulted in the loss of individuals' right to their property. The War on Drugs and War on Crime have resulted in the loss of individual rights to security of person, such as habeas corpus, due process, and the right to be presumed innocent until proven guilty. They also gave the government new power to seize property from the accused before they are found guilty of anything. Freezing bank accounts and confiscating property based merely upon an indictment is characterized by the government as being "tough on crime." But what about those who are eventually found not guilty? Prosecutions typically take years. The families of the accused are literally held hostage by the government without access to their money and with a substantial portion of their property confiscated. These tactics inhibit the ability of the accused to mount a defense. These tactics clearly violate the intention of the Fifth Amendment, which states that no one will be "be deprived of life, liberty, or property, without due process of law."[3]

The media and popular culture constantly promote a message that crime is out of control and more drastic measures are needed to fight it. Yet, how many of us have ever actually been the victim of a violent crime, or even know anyone who has? In cities of millions, local news will run the story of a murder over and over until they have created an illusion that the one murder they have covered was twenty or thirty. This is not to imply it is an intentional strategy to scare people. Most who have worked in television news are familiar with the slogan, "If it bleeds, it leads." Regardless of the intentions, the result is still the same. The public is misled into thinking an emergency exists and they are in immediate danger. They then employ emergency reasoning regarding their rights.

The campaign does not end with the news. Consider the average police drama on television or in the movies. Most carry the same message. The law enforcement community is fighting a valiant but losing "war" against rampant crime. The rights of the accused are preventing law enforcement officers from saving us from these dangerous criminals. Anyone forming their opinions about the justice system from these dramas would conclude that an alarming number of dangerous criminals escape justice "on a technicality" because of those troublesome constitutional protections. How often does the heroic cop say with unmasked resentment, "The accused has rights?" The clear message to the viewer: constitutional protections are preventing law enforcement from protecting you from dangerous people during this War on Crime emergency. They are arresting the perpetrators, but constitutional protections are allowing most of them to "walk."

This is completely contradicted by reality. In the real world, those accused of crimes have very little chance of getting an acquittal, especially if they are indicted in federal court. With the erosion of constitutional protections resulting from years of elected representatives attempting to be "tougher on crime," the conviction rates have skyrocketed. According to the U.S. Department of Justice, the conviction rate in federal court in 2005 was 90%.[4]

Here is just one example. Most Americans are familiar with the rule of evidence against hearsay. This prohibits a third party from testifying to a conversation he or she was not a party to. In other words, I cannot testify in court that I heard Joe tell Mary that he was going to commit a crime. This is a crucial protection for defendants, because a third party can easily take the conversation out of context and cannot be effectively cross examined on the background or context of the conversation. If the witness is lying, there is no way to expose it, as they can merely stand on the assertion, "That's what I heard."

This protection is revoked when the defendant is accused of a conspiracy. In those cases, the government claims it cannot prove its case without hearsay testimony. The rule allowing hearsay in conspiracy cases was originally put in place to prosecute organized crime figures. It was considered vital to the case against a mafia leader that the former member of his "family" who now testified against him could testify that the accused had given orders to commit crimes. Few argued against eliminating this protection for the accused when it could help convict a mafia godfather. However, once that right was surrendered for the mafia figure, it was surrendered for all.

As a result, the government now includes a charge of conspiracy in virtually every case it prosecutes. Further, prosecution witnesses have often plead guilty themselves and must give "helpful" testimony in order to lessen their own sentences. Since the government can now allow these witnesses to give hearsay testimony, the witnesses can testify to hearing the accused say whatever the government wants them to have heard. If you do not believe this goes on in our sacrosanct justice system, you are fooling yourself at your own peril.

In addition to infringing rights during trial, the War on Crime has tainted the administration of justice at sentencing. Under the pretense of making sentencing fairer to minorities and more uniform in courts in different parts of the country, a rigid set of sentencing guidelines has been established, especially in federal court, to which judges must adhere in administering sentencing.[5] These guidelines assign point totals to various crimes, with adjustments up or down depending upon mitigating factors. Most add points for factors that are considered to make the offense more egregious, while a few subtract points for factors such as acceptance of responsibility or cooperation with the authorities. Based upon the point total, the judge must then sentence within a narrow range associated with that point total in the guidelines.[6]

Therefore, regardless of the judge's impression of the case or what reasons he might have for being more lenient to the defendant, he must give the defendant at least the minimum sentence prescribed for that point total. In most cases, the sentencing minimums are not significantly lower than the maximums.

It gets worse. In determining sentence, the judge is also required to consider "other relevant conduct," which not only includes crimes the defendant was convicted of, but also those the defendant was charged with and acquitted of. The judge is even required to consider conduct the defendant was not charged with at all!

Suppose a defendant is charged with one count of conspiracy and seven individual counts of a particular crime. Even if the defendant is acquitted of all but one of the individual counts, the court will nevertheless assign points based upon the one count the defendant was convicted of, the six individual counts and the one conspiracy count, even though the defendant was acquitted of all but the first. Moreover, any additional evidence of conduct by the defendant that was presented by the prosecution, even if it was not the substance of a specific charge and regardless of the fact that it might have been totally discredited by the defense, is also assigned points. In addition, even though the defendant was acquitted of the conspiracy, points can be assigned for the conduct of all members of it, including participants the defendant never met. Once these inflated point totals are tallied, the resulting jail sentence is inevitably far longer than the crime warrants.

These sentencing guidelines work together with tainted rules of evidence to incarcerate vast numbers of Americans for what used to be considered relatively minor crimes. To explain all this "American Holocaust" would take many volumes. However, just consider how these two examples work together.

A government witness facing sentencing himself is called to testify against a defendant charged with conspiracy. Remember that the witness' downward point adjustments depend on his testimony being helpful to the prosecution. The hearsay rules are suspended, so the witness can testify to conversations he claims he heard the defendant have with other people. He testifies to three conversations during which he says he heard the defendant talk about selling one kilo, two kilos, and three kilos of cocaine, respectively. The amount of drugs in a drug conspiracy case also carries points, so the more drugs involved in the crime, the more points assigned to the defendant. Those six kilos are now assigned points and counted during sentencing, even if there is no other proof those kilos existed and the witness' testimony was completely discredited by the defense.

In addition, if the witness testifies about conversations he overheard involving other members of the conspiracy, even among members the defendant never met and related to crimes for which the defendant has not been charged, any kilos mentioned in regard to those conversations will also be added to the defendant's point total. This is how a drug user caught with a few grams of cocaine for personal use can end up in prison for 20 years for "drug trafficking." Rather than an extreme example of how the system could be abused, this is business as usual in our American courts. For financial crimes, substitute the amount of dollars for the amount of drugs and all of the same rules apply.

The perception that the guilty go free because they have too many constitutional protections couldn't be farther from the truth. On the contrary, the vast numbers of Americans imprisoned suggests the innocent are imprisoned at a much greater rate than the guilty are freed.

According to the U.S. Department of Justice, there were close to 2.3 million people incarcerated in the United States as of June 30, 2007.[7] That is more than 1 in every 100 adults. Both in total numbers and in percentage of population, the United States incarcerates more of its citizens than any nation in the world, including the supposedly more oppressive People's Republic of China (they have about 1.5 million in jail out of a population 4 times as large as the U.S.). Unless the American people are the most depraved that ever lived, we are clearly doing something very wrong. If there is any emergency related to crime in the United States, it is the out of control justice system itself.

While the prison populations in the various states have finally started decreasing during the past few years, the federal prison population is increasing more. This means not only is the overall number of Americans incarcerated continuing to increase, but the federal government is assuming more and more jurisdiction previously reserved to the states. Both of these trends are ominous. They will not reverse while the War on Crime continues.

The infringement of rights of the accused or convicted does not end with their release from prison. For the rest of their lives, those convicted of felonies are not allowed to exercise rights that are supposed to be inalienable. Regardless of the nature of the crime, convicted felons are prohibited from bearing arms, making them permanently dependent upon government for defense. They are prohibited from holding many licenses or gaining access to secured areas. In many states, they lose their right to vote and can only regain it after an onerous process which may or may not be successful.

Even for a crime as innocuous as tax evasion, which some people commit as a means of civil disobedience or protest, they lose many rights forever. By elevating more and more crimes to felony status and convicting more and more Americans every year, a significant percentage of the population is becoming a second class of citizen with far fewer rights. While there are 2.3 million Americans in jail right now, there is a much larger group with a past felony conviction. That number could be in the tens of millions.

All of these intolerable results are a direct result of the "state of emergency" mindset. The culmination of this thinking is the Global War on Terror. This is the "mother of all wars" as far as government infringement of rights is concerned. It is like the War on Crime on steroids. As alarming as are the disadvantages to defendants in civilian courts, the War on Terror may deprive a defendant of any day in court whatsoever. As a result of the Patriot Act, the Military Commission Act of 2006, and certain executive orders issued by President Bush (who is not supposed to be able to make laws at all), the possibility exists for American citizens to be arrested and imprisoned without recourse to challenge their arrest in court. If they are deemed an "enemy combatant" by the executive branch, they can be held indefinitely without being charged and perhaps even subjected to torture.

President Obama now says he can even kill suspected terrorists without due process. With a more terrifying "emergency" comes more terrifying government measures to combat it.

Not only is this alleged emergency infinitely more terrifying than your average mugging or car theft, but its scope is unlimited. The terrorists can be anywhere in the world. Therefore, government not only claims authority to violate the rights of its own citizens, but of citizens of other nations. Until the worldwide emergency is over, no individual and no nation is safe from the next "preventative" measure the government will employ. These include invading a foreign nation even when no acts of war have been committed or war declared, so long as that nation is perceived as a threat to security.

Contrary to the claim that "the world changed on September 11, 2001," the Global War on Terror is not without precedent. In fact, most authoritarian societies became that way because of measures taken to protect the population against some ominous threat invoked by its government. The parallels between present-day America and one such society are downright terrifying. That society was Nazi Germany. Consider the similarities.

Prior to Adolf Hitler's ascension to power in Germany, there was an historic collapse of the currency, in large part due to unsustainable economic policies. As has America today, Germany responded by ceding more and more power to its central government. Hitler was viewed as "a man who could get things done," as all of our recent presidential candidates have touted themselves.

Just like 21st century America, Germany experienced a spectacular terrorist attack, the Reichstag Fire. It was used by the central government to violate the civil liberties of its people. Germany's Reichstag Fire Act and Enabling Act were direct parallels to America's Patriot Act and Military Commissions Act. Habeas corpus was abolished. Just as they have in modern America, the economic policies of the authoritarian government proved unsustainable. When another currency collapse was imminent, Hitler set out to plunder the gold of Europe to back the failing currency.

As in Germany of the 1930's, an appeal to patriotism is used to persuade Americans to support greater intrusion into their lives by government and more warfare abroad. Any dissent is labeled as unpatriotic. Police state oppression of political dissent hangs over America like a dark cloud. Like the Nazis, the U.S. government invaded a country that did not attack it and is threatening to expand its wars of aggression into Iran and elsewhere. Slowly, even establishment media is starting to speculate that the true reason for doing so is to "secure resources." America may be attempting to solve its inherent economic problems by plundering the wealth of other nations.

The Federal Emergency Management Administration (FEMA) is completing projects to build prison camps throughout the United States with the capacity to detain millions of people.[8] Most of these camps are already staffed and standing empty. Who will be imprisoned in them? FEMA also procured over 500,000 plastic coffins which are stored in plain view at a roadside in Georgia. What are they preparing for?

In October 2008, the U.S. Army's 3rd Infantry Division's 1st Brigade Combat Team was recalled from Iraq and assigned to active duty within the United States. According to the Army Times, this is "the first time an active unit has been given a dedicated assignment to NorthCom, a joint command established in 2002 to provide command and control for federal homeland defense efforts and coordinate defense support of civil authorities."[9] The article goes on to say,

"They may be called upon to help with civil unrest and crowd control or to deal with potentially horrific scenarios such as massive poisoning and chaos in response to a chemical, biological, radiological, nuclear or high-yield explosive, or CBRNE, attack."

This report did not come from an internet conspiracy theory website. It appeared in the Army Times, the official publication of the U.S. Army. The founders' fear of "standing armies" has become a reality.

In Hitler's Germany, the regular army was augmented by a citizen paramilitary force of teenagers and young adults popularly known as the "Hitler Youth." In a speech in Colorado Springs, CO on July 2, 2008, Barack Obama said,

"We cannot continue to rely only on our military in order to achieve the national security objectives that we've set. We've got to have a civilian national security force that's just as powerful, just as strong, just as well funded." [10]

Curiously, although video of the speech confirms that Obama made this statement; all known transcripts of the speech provided by his campaign omit it.

Most would argue that anything similar to Nazi Germany is impossible in the United States. This is a very naïve perspective. No German of 1929 could have imagined the nightmare they would be living in ten years later. Most Germans did not want it, nor would they support the abominable policies of the Nazis.

One could certainly argue that all of the federal government policies cited above have far different intentions than Hitler had. This is a very dangerous way to look at it. Hitler did not elicit the cheers of millions by telling them he was going to oppress them. Just like in America today, everything he did was viewed by his citizens as a temporary measure to react to the current emergency. It was not until years after they had lost their freedom that they realized the emergency was never going to end. By then, it was too late.

Unless the American people put a stop to it, the Global War on Terror is never going to end. In addition to it being impossible to win (to ensure that no terrorist act is ever committed by anyone anywhere ever again), the War on Terror perpetuates itself. Since prosecuting it includes invading foreign nations, there is constant motive provided for new terrorist activity. While the United States remains virtually invincible on the battlefield, there is little recourse for those who object to U.S. armies of occupation other than guerrilla or terrorist tactics. That is not meant to condone or legitimize terrorism. However, the reality is those who practice it are perpetually motivated by the War on Terror itself.

Domestic wars may also combine with the Global War on Terror to produce even worse results. The economic crisis has already resulted in government seizure of unwarranted power to combat the "economic emergency." Massive new regulations and other interventions into the economy have been instituted to combat problems caused by previous interventions. This government "cure," which is far worse than the disease, could eventually result in massive shortages of basic necessities like food, water, and gasoline. That could lead to civil unrest and very easily bring on martial law, necessitating exercise of all of the frightening powers described above. The phony emergencies could very well create a real one.

The only true emergency Americans face is the unwarranted accumulation of power by their government. That accumulation is accelerating and only needs the proper crisis to provide an excuse for the government to use it. This is not a new or unique scenario. It has happened countless times throughout history. In every case, the citizens told themselves, "It can never happen here."

We must decide we will no longer acknowledge a permanent state of emergency and demand that the various wars end. This does not mean we no longer punish crime or offer ourselves up as sitting ducks to terrorists. On the contrary, we should protect our rights to life, liberty, and property, but without at the same time destroying those rights. We must bring government back under our control as an obedient servant, rather than a tyrannical master. This aspect of the America Crisis is more urgent than any other. Unless we wake up and take a stand against these infringements of our rights soon, we may lose the ability to exercise them forever.

Chapter 11
The Media Monolith

"You know well that that government always kept a kind of standing army of news writers who without any regard to truth, or to what should be like truth, invented & put into the papers whatever might serve the minister. This suffices with the mass of the people who have no means of distinguishing the false from the true paragraphs of a newspaper."

– Thomas Jefferson[1]

Never before has news traveled faster around the world than it does today. Satellite and internet technologies make it possible for people in the United States to watch events occurring in China in real time. Newspapers from all over the world are now published online in several languages, almost all including English, allowing access to news from every continent. In addition, there is also unprecedented motivation to want to know what is happening in remote parts of the world, due to our increasingly globalized economy. As is often said, the world is getting smaller every day.

With media outlets utilizing these new capabilities to bring us news 24/7, one would assume the average American today is much better informed than his counterpart fifty or one hundred years ago. The media would certainly have us believe that. However, the increased quantity of news coverage has not necessarily resulted in increased quality. In fact, any objective analysis of 21st century news coverage in the United States would have to conclude

Americans are grossly misinformed. This is due to lack of coverage of vital news stories and distorted coverage that "spins" the news for the benefit of interested parties.

First, consider some stories most major media outlets failed to cover. On November 13, 2000, a short piece appeared in Time Magazine reporting that Saddam Hussein had announced he would no longer accept U.S. dollars for Iraqi oil.[2] The article was a mere 3 paragraphs long and seems to be the only U.S. news coverage of this announcement. For three years afterwards, Iraqi oil was traded in euros, until U.S. forces invaded Iraq and deposed Hussein. One of the first official actions of the new interim government was to restore the U.S. dollar as the unit of exchange for Iraqi oil.

Some have claimed Hussein's change to euros, which he announced immediately after the election of George W. Bush, was the primary reason for the U.S. invasion of Iraq. They argue that since the U.S. dollar went off the gold standard in 1971, it has retained its value as the world's reserve currency largely because the majority of the world's oil sales are made in U.S. dollars. Any government deciding to trade oil in another currency would be a threat to the dollar.

Former Treasury Secretary Paul O'Neill claimed an invasion of Iraq was discussed at President Bush's first cabinet meeting, several months before September 11, 2001. If true, then the invasion was obviously motivated by something other than the 9/11 attacks.

Whether alternative theories about the Bush administration's motivations for invading Iraq are true or not, one thing is certain. Hussein's decision to cease accepting U.S. dollars for his oil was newsworthy and almost no media outlets covered it. The Bush administration was not questioned even by media that tend to be liberally biased, not even to give the administration a chance to refute such claims. To this day, most Americans are not aware Hussein made this decision or that the U.S. reversed it immediately upon taking control of the Iraqi government.

While this may seem like the stuff of conspiracy theories, it is not the last chapter in this story of oil and the U.S. dollar. A few years later, this same pattern would repeat itself. Unreported in the U.S. news media, the Iranian government announced in 2004 that it would not only begin converting its oil sales to euros, but that it would launch a new exchange, called the Iranian Oil Bourse, to compete with the two established exchanges trading oil in U.S. dollars.[3] Currently, the New York Mercantile Exchange (NYMEX) in New York and the International Petroleum Exchange (IPE) in London dominate the worldwide oil markets. Both exchanges support oil trades exclusively in U.S. dollars.

The Iranian Oil Bourse is a major news story, regardless of any connection to the Bush administration's saber rattling towards Iran. Yet, despite that Iran's announcement to create it has been reported in media outlets all over the world since 2004, the U.S. media is conspicuously silent on it. Why? It is hard to dismiss as coincidence that the Bush administration's condemnation of Iran's nuclear program and increasing threats of war began to escalate immediately after Iran made this announcement.

If you are skeptical, then consider a third nation that made a major announcement regarding selling their oil in euros. In December of 2006, the BBC reported that Venezuela had "expressed interest in an Iranian move to ask buyers to pay for oil in Euros rather than US dollars."[4] True, Hugo Chavez had been a target of the Bush administration for many years by that point. The U.S. may have been secretly involved in the failed coup attempt in Venezuela in 2002. However, the correlation between this announcement and amplified belligerence by the U.S. government is hard to write off as mere coincidence, especially considering the similarity to Iran and Iraq.

Whether or not the Iraq War was connected to oil and the U.S. dollar, these decisions by world leaders were major news stories. They were reported by media outlets all over the world, but not in the United States. The Bush administration has never had to refute any allegations regarding oil and the dollar being connected to the Iraq War because no reporter has ever even asked. This represents either journalistic ineptitude on a colossal scale or a deliberate effort to keep this issue from the public.

This is only one of many major news stories the American media is conspicuously silent on. However, failing to report news Americans would consider vitally important is only one way in which the media fails the public. The other major failing is distortion of the issues they do report. Often, stories are "framed" in a way that affects public perception, rather than objectively reporting and exploring all possible angles of the story.

The Iraq War provides another example. There was lively media debate in the months leading up to the war. On the surface, it might even appear the media had challenged the Bush administration's case for war vigorously. However, the "debate" about the justification for this war was framed into whether Iraq possessed "weapons of mass destruction" or "constituted a threat to the United States."

No reporter challenged the administration on the grounds that no state of war existed between Iraq and the United States. No reporter questioned the administration on how they justified using U.S. troops without a formal declaration of war. Most of the industrialized nations of the world pose a greater threat to the U.S. than Iraq, even if Iraq had the weapons the Bush administration said they did. Why invade Iraq and not nations that posed a greater threat? These and many other questions needed to be asked of the administration and not one member of the American media asked them. Why?

More recently, during the debates on the bailout legislation, the same framing occurred. The criticism of the proposed bill was limited to discussion of executive bonuses, "helping Wall Street but not Main Street," the effect on the stock market, or restoring confidence to the credit markets. Not one reporter seemed interested in the property rights question. Where did the government derive the authority to use taxpayer money this way?

While the questions the media did raise could be debated, no defense of the bailouts was possible from a property rights perspective. This bailout represented legal plunder in the first degree, yet not one reporter even broached the issue. Certainly, these are not outlandish questions. Why did not one news reporter ask them of our government?

Once you recognize this tendency to limit debates in the government's favor, it becomes apparent everywhere. Never does the media seem interested in championing the rights of the individual against the state. Always we here the same tired refrain. "The government had to do something."

Within this framework, Americans are lead into one no win situation after another and asked to choose. How can Medicare and Social Security be reformed? Tax increases or a decrease in benefits? Perhaps raising the age of eligibility? Never "Should they be abolished or phased out?" When an odd dissenter broaches troublesome questions, they are made to appear ridiculous by the host or the "panel of experts."

Quite often, these experts are making spurious arguments or resorting to ad hominem, but the power of the broadcast overcomes the ability of most people to distinguish between true, substantive arguments and spin. Having never been taught the first principles in school, nor educated in logic or rhetoric, it never occurs to most Americans to consider any other alternatives than those served up to them by the machine.

The obvious question is "Why?" Why do our media outlets consistently mislead us? How did our free press become little more than propagandists for the government? Is it a massive conspiracy? The media outlets are all privately owned. Is the free market is to blame?

Before attempting to answer the question of "why" the media does what it does, it is imperative to answer a prerequisite question: Who is the media?

Increasingly, it is a very short list of international corporations. For decades, there has been consolidation in the media industry, resulting in a small group of corporations controlling most media and entertainment in the developed world. These companies control not only the news, but a large percentage of the entertainment industry, including television, film, and music. As a result, the message broadcasted over all of these media has become increasingly uniform.

Often the free market is blamed for this, when it is actually a result of the same systemic risk/regulation dynamic discussed in Chapter 5. The massive regulatory structure insulates these companies from competition, supposedly intended to protect consumers. In reality, it makes it difficult for new or smaller competitors to enter the market. When regulations that prohibit consolidation are relaxed, leaving the rest of the regulations in place, massive consolidation follows. That leaves a small group of companies, insulated from competition, with a vested interest in promoting a positive image of their protector, the government.

It should come as no surprise that this dynamic has its roots in (what else) the New Deal. The seminal legislation is the Communications Act of 1934, which was later overhauled by the Telecommunications Act of 1996.[5] While some details have changed and updates were made in the 1990's with new developments in technology, the underlying principle remains the same. The government controls the airwaves and decides which companies will get which opportunities. It then tries to mitigate the negative consequences of its interference in the market with another regulatory agency, the Federal Communications Commission (FCC).

As in other markets, the result is a never-ending cycle of government-created problems which the government tries to control with increasingly prohibitive regulation. Eventually, politicians friendly to the large corporations get into office and roll back only those regulations that keep them from using their artificial advantage to monopolize the market, while leaving the rest of the regulatory structure in place. The public then blames deregulation for the resulting oligopoly, forgetting how the corporations achieved it.

The news and entertainment media industry is no different than any other. The only way to produce the best products at the lowest prices for consumers is to let market forces work and respect property rights. Government control has had its chance for seventy years. It has failed. The airwaves should be taken back from the government and returned to the people. The time has come to restore our media industry with freedom.

Chapter 12
False Prophets of Freedom

"Which is better—to be ruled by one tyrant three thousand miles away, or by three thousand tyrants not a mile away?"

– Mather Byles, Sr. (1770)[1]

Like liberty, tyranny is a concept most people think they understand, but don't. In school, we are taught about "freedom fighters" throughout history, but not what freedom really is. Likewise, we are rarely educated on what the nature of tyranny is.

We are led to believe the tyrants of history were just evil people who committed their crimes merely for the sake of making people miserable. While this may explain the motivations of the villains in children's comic books, it is not an accurate depiction of life in the real world. In the real world, people usually commit crimes for some type of gain. This is not different when the criminal is a head of state. Here in the real world, there is usually only one motivation for tyranny: plunder.

No conqueror in history went to the expense and trouble of raising, training, and feeding an army, marching them across vast distances, and risking his own position and wealth merely to suppress free speech. Nor have they done so merely to infringe freedom of religion, freedom of the press, or the right of the people to freely assemble. Attacking these rights are only a means to an end. The end has always been plunder. Virtually every tyrant that ever lived ultimately had the same objective: to gather wealth he did not earn.

If you definition of liberty ends at freedom of speech, freedom of religion, freedom of association, and the right to due process, then you are omitting the heart and soul of liberty: property rights. Without them, there is no freedom, no matter how fiercely the "civil liberties" are protected.

Legal plunder by government generally falls into two categories: welfare and warfare. While cosmetically different, they are essentially the same. They represent the use of government force to plunder the property of the individual. One merely does it farther away than the other, a relatively minor difference.

Bastiat said there are only three alternatives for a society in determining how to address the question of plunder. Let us look at these three alternatives again, this time inserting political parties next to the alternative they advocate:

1. When the few plunder the many. (Republicans)

2. When everybody plunders everybody (Democrats)

3. When nobody plunders anybody (Freedom – the position of neither party)[2]

Like the unfortunate child in the middle of a game of "pickle in the middle," Americans have been running back and forth between the first two alternatives offered by their political parties for decades. It has never occurred to the majority that neither one can benefit them in the end. There are only two possible reasons for this. Either people do not understand property rights or they do not want to understand, because they believe they benefit from the plunder. The second possibility is more pathetic than the first. Like the gamblers in Las Vegas, they should know by now that the House always wins.

Rather than objecting to legal plunder itself, false prophets of freedom argue the loot should merely be divided up differently. Democrats object to corporate welfare and tax cuts, but promise free healthcare and higher minimum wages. Republicans object to food stamps and Big Bird, but promise corporate farm subsidies and defense contracts.

In the end, politicians can be bought with votes. If the majority of voters demand cuts, they'd get them. However, when the majority of voters demand that the government give them other people's property, then it becomes clear why Madison described democracy as "the most vile form of government."[3]

If you are against the war in Iraq, but go on to say the money we are spending on that war should instead be spent on providing healthcare to uninsured Americans, you are not against legal plunder. You merely want to divide up the loot differently.

If you are opposed to the recent bailouts of the banks during the mortgage crisis, but go on to say the government should instead help average Americans in danger of losing their homes, you are not against legal plunder. You merely want to divide up the loot differently.

If you are against the fascist alliance between large corporations and government, but suggest taxing the profits of corporations more heavily to fund some other redistribution of wealth, you are not against legal plunder. You merely want to divide up the loot differently.

If you are concerned Social Security and Medicare are imminently insolvent, and go on to argue that they must be "reformed," rather than abolished or phased out, then you are not against legal plunder. You are merely concerned that you won't get your share of the loot.

These are only a few examples of the flawed logic promoted by false prophets of freedom. Presently, average Americans are running from the Republicans (the few plunder the many) to the Democrats (everybody plunders everybody) in their perennial game of pickle in the middle. They still haven't noticed that no matter which side they run to, they never actually succeed in catching the ball. This is leading in an ominous direction.

After systematically destroying property rights for more than a century, the inevitable end to which such a society comes is near. The government monster Americans have built is now attacking the civil liberties as well. The police state measures and perpetual war are not departures by the Bush and Obama administrations but the inevitable result of decades of legal plunder. This was Hayek's central point in *The Road to Serfdom*. Nazism was the natural result of socialism and England's socialism of the 1940's would eventually lead to the same results. In Hayek's own words,

"Most planners who have seriously considered the practical aspects of their task have little doubt that a directed economy must be run on more or less dictatorial lines."[4]

There will be no restoration of liberty in America until Americans understand the true nature of freedom and tyranny. Until Americans restore protection of property rights, freedom will continue to elude us.

Do not look to politicians to offer you Bastiat's third alternative. Politicians have always seduced people with promises of other people's money, while keeping the majority of the loot for themselves. It is left up to every American to reject false prophets of freedom, regardless of the letters after their names.

Chapter 13
Extremism in the Defense of Liberty

"Is life so dear, or peace so sweet, as to be purchased at the price of chains and slavery? Forbid it, Almighty God! I know not what course others may take, but as for me, give me liberty, or give me death!"

– Patrick Henry (1775)[1]

"Don't go to extremes." What could be sounder, more reasonable advice? Moderation is extolled everywhere as a virtue. Drink in moderation. Enjoy good food in moderation. Pursue personal interests in moderation. Too much of a good thing can be just as bad for you as poison. Moderation is "the silken string running through the pearl chain of all virtues,"[2] said Joseph Hall.

In civics classes, we are taught that "democracy" functions based upon compromise. Compromise is the only way conflicting interests can exist together peacefully. Moderation is unselfish. It respects the interest of all parties. It is willing to "give and take." Moderation is fairness.

On the website http://moderaterepublican.net, Moderate Republicans are described as believing:

"...that government does have a basic social responsibility to help those in need; a belief that the nation does have international responsibilities."

"Moderate lawmakers are consensus builders. But then again the art of legislating is that of compromise, negotiation, and recognition that other views have merit. This does not mean Moderates compromise core values, but rather they understand the complexities of passing intelligent legislation that benefits the greater good."

"Moderates were the first internationalists. The nation, they contended, had a critical role to play in advancing democracy in the world."

This platform is not substantially different than Democratic President Woodrow Wilson's in 1912. Yet, this was without question the platform of George Bush and the most recent incarnation of the Republican Party. The so-called "neo-conservatives" are moderate Republicans. What could be wrong with that?

The media often describes American politics today as "extremely polarized." Yet, any objective analysis of American politics would conclude the debate is now between centrist, moderate Republicans and ultra-liberal, socialist Democrats. What is common to both is a belief in an enormously powerful, monolithic government that reaches into every aspect of its constituent's lives and asserts its power over every corner of the earth.

President Bush and the Republicans passed Medicare Part D, increasing entitlement spending more than any administration since LBJ. President Obama and the Democrats passed the Affordable Care Act ("Obamacare"). Both parties started new wars in the Middle East and expanded civil liberties violations at home. Individual liberty is completely off the table. How did we get here?

Extolling the virtues of moderation has played a major role. When it comes to wine, women, and song, a little moderation is a very healthy thing. When it comes to questions of liberty, it is a deadly poison. If liberty is one extreme and slavery the other, how could we ever benefit from a compromise? Reflecting on the choices we've been offered over the past 100 years, we have constantly had to choose between giving up a little liberty or giving up a great deal. Government never proposes to get smaller or surrender any control. When a new government program or initiative is proposed, the choices never include more liberty. At best, moderation carries the day, a compromise is reached, and only a little liberty is lost. However, the next debate starts from there.

It is clear why a government seeking more control would extol the virtues of moderation and compromise. When it comes to the government and liberty, moderation is like the old saying, "Heads I win, tails you lose." Extremism is an easy position to vilify. Nobody likes an extremist. Note how the rhetoric by supporters of the "Global War on Terror" has shifted imperceptibly from "terrorists" to "extremists."

It was the "neo-con" moderate Republican platform that Barry Goldwater opposed and defeated in the 1964 Republican presidential primaries. Why did he lose? He was characterized as an extremist, a label he welcomed, saying,

"Let me remind you that extremism in the defense of liberty is no vice, and let me remind you also that moderation in the pursuit of justice is no virtue."

Critics of any movement advocating individual liberty immediately label those movements "extremist." The most common obfuscations are "it is too dangerous to let everyone do whatever they want," or "no government at all is not practical," as if either of these arguments were being made. This tactic is effective because it exploits the emotional impact of the word "extremism" and counts on a public that will hear it and accept the rest without critical analysis. No one ever considers that perhaps extremism in the defense of liberty is a virtue.

Perhaps the only way to achieve liberty is to reject moderation and compromise altogether. As crazy as that may sound at first, a little reflection reveals otherwise. If liberty means never to initiate the use of force, what is the moderate position? Initiating a little force? If liberty means taking the product of someone's labor without his consent is stealing, what is an acceptable compromise? Stealing a little? If liberty means a person's life is his own to do with as he wishes, as long as he does not violate the rights of others, what does the moderate say? Is his life only partly his own? Before rejecting extremism in the defense of liberty, ask yourself: Do we really want liberty in moderation?

Liberty in moderation is what we have attempted. It is the ideology behind the "mixed economy." It has failed. Let us practice moderation in the indulgence of our appetites, but let us be extremists in the defense of liberty.

Chapter 14
The Road to Freedom

"We have it in our power to begin the world over again."

– Thomas Paine (1776)[1]

By now, if this short book has adequately explained the principles America was founded upon, the reader is beginning to realize just how far we have departed from those principles. Almost every aspect of our government violates the individual rights it was originally constructed to protect. As a result, virtually all of our societal problems are caused by government. The subsequent government solutions only exacerbate those problems, or cause new ones that are even worse. We are in a downward spiral both economically and socially with an ever-increasing loss of peace, prosperity, and freedom.

This downward spiral manifests itself in the increasing extent to which America finds itself ensnarled in wars that do not end, economic malaise, and an emerging police state that purports to protect Americans from the "new dangers of the 21st century." We are literally on Hayek's Road to Serfdom, exactly as he predicted we would travel it.

It is not inevitable that we continue down this road. At any moment, Americans can decide to reject the false choices offered by their politicians and make their own choices, forcing the government back to being a servant of the people, instead of an increasingly tyrannical master. We can, as the man who inspired this book wrote, begin the world over again.

If we are going to do so, we must recognize the root cause of our problems instead of arguing about the various symptoms. We must realize that we did not lose our freedom and prosperity due to mistakes made by particular leaders or political parties. Instead, it was a fundamental change in philosophy that led to the decline. Specifically, we abandoned our belief in the sovereignty of the individual over the state and exalted the state over the individual. This is the foundation of all of the destructive policies that have brought us to where we are right now.

One indication of this philosophical change has been the linguistic shift in referring to the United States as a "democracy," rather than a republic. There are fundamental differences between a pure democracy, which is absolute rule by a majority, and a constitutional republic, which limits the power of the majority over the individual. The real turning point came at the beginning of the 20th century. As Benedict LaRosa writes,

"Widespread use of the term democracy began with the Woodrow Wilson administration in 1912. It was during this administration that the anti-republican amendments – the 16th (income tax) and 17th (popular election of senators) – were added to our Constitution and a central bank – the Federal Reserve – was established. All three acts centralized power."[2]

Not coincidentally, the Wilson administration sowed the seeds for the two institutions that have become the greatest burden on American society: the welfare and warfare states. Wilson's "progressive" ideas about economic policy and his commitment to "make the world safe for democracy" represented fundamental changes to the mission of the United States government. No longer was its mission to secure individual rights. In fact, individual rights were now secondary to societal goals of a more equitable distribution of wealth and worldwide democracy, imposed by U.S. military might. Here were the seeds of today's enormous entitlement programs and equally enormous military budget.

As the founders warned us, democracy is not freedom, nor is the democratic process any guarantee of freedom. It is simply the best way we have come up with for the people to choose their representatives. Democracy must be restrained so that it does not destroy individual rights, which it is prone to do. One should look upon those who continually refer to the United States as a "democracy" with a healthy suspicion of their understanding of liberty, their motives, or both.

Any solution to our current problems must begin with another change of philosophy. We must again elevate the rights of the individual above the power of the state. We must recognize the folly of trying to use government coercion to try to create domestic equality or world peace. Force is only justified in defense and the government is nothing more than the collective use of force. Legitimizing force for anything other than self-defense inherently makes slaves of us all.

We must take responsibility for our problems. In a monarchy or dictatorship, one might lay the blame at the feet of government alone and simply argue for its removal. In the United States, we are that government. Some argue we are really ruled by an oligarchy of wealthy elitists, but if that is true, who gave them that power? In many ways, it has not been a despotic government refusing to respect our wishes that has ruined us. Rather, the government has grown despotic *because* it has given us what we asked it for. This, too, was anticipated by the founders. In the words of James Madison,

"Wherever the real power in a Government lies, there is the danger of oppression. In our Government, the real power lies in the majority of the Community, and the invasion of private rights is chiefly to be apprehended, not from acts of government contrary to the sense of its constituents, but from acts in which the Government is the mere instrument of the major number of Constituents."[3]

We have asked government to solve problems it is ill-suited to solve and destroyed our liberty in the process. We asked it to prevent bank failures and we got a despotic central bank. We asked it to provide healthcare and a comfortable retirement and we got crippling entitlement programs that threaten to bankrupt us. We asked it to fight a "war on drugs" and we put millions of Americans in prison. In each case, we failed to see that when force is used other than to protect life, liberty, and property, it must necessarily attack them. By violating a moral law, we have achieved disastrous practical results. If there is a transcendent justice in the universe, here is proof of its existence.

Whether we were duped into selling our freedom by some secret conspiracy or whether it was just plain old human nature doesn't really matter. What matters is that all of our current afflictions of government require our continued consent and cooperation. Once we decide we no longer want this type of government, we have the power to "alter or abolish it" almost immediately.

There is a simple solution to almost every issue we face. That does not mean the solutions will be painless. We have been undermining our liberty for over a century. The adjustment, especially in the case of economic policy, will require some temporary sacrifice. The alternative is unsustainable. We can either choose to end the American empire and restore the American republic, or continue down the road to serfdom and eventual collapse. That is the end of all empires.

What is more important than exactly how we get there is that we figure out where we are trying to go. Right now, Americans are demanding more socialism. Politicians encourage this by deflecting the blame for economic problems away from the government.

It is actually socialism that results in the concentration of wealth in a small percentage of the population. Once Americans reject legal plunder, the entire house of cards will fall. It is quite a different vision for America to be without institutions that we have come to think of as facts of life, like Social Security, Medicare, and a massive, international military force. What we must realize is that it will be a better America, a freer America, and a sustainable America. It will be a reawakening of liberty.

Once this reawakening has taken place, we must understand the political means to achieving our goals. In a nation ruled by laws, it is the laws themselves that must be changed, and bad laws that must be repealed. Too often, Americans are distracted by the pageantry surrounding the presidential elections, and forget that the president doesn't make any of the laws that either protect or harm them. To be sure, the executive branch uses its visibility to influence the legislature, but ultimately it must ask Congress to change the laws.

While the Patriot Act, Military Commissions Act, and other unpopular laws are often associated with the Bush Administration, Congress had to vote those laws into existence. The executive branch has no power to compel legislators. The Constitution puts the legislative power exclusively into the hands of the people's elected representatives. That does not guarantee liberty. As Madison put it,

"In a government where numerous and extensive prerogatives are placed in the hands of a hereditary monarch, the executive department is very justly regarded as the source of danger, and watched with all the jealousy which a zeal for liberty ought to inspire. In a democracy, where a multitude of people exercise in person the legislative functions, and are continually exposed, by their incapacity for regular deliberation and concerted measures, to the ambitious intrigues of their executive magistrates, tyranny may well be apprehended, on some favorable emergency, to start up in the same quarter. But in a representative republic, where the executive magistracy is carefully limited; both in the extent and the duration of its power; and where the legislative power is exercised by an assembly, which is inspired, by a supposed influence over the people, with an intrepid confidence in its own strength; which is sufficiently numerous to feel all the passions which actuate a multitude, yet not so numerous as to be incapable of pursuing the objects of its passions, by means which reason prescribes; it is against the enterprising ambition of this department that the people ought to indulge all their jealousy and exhaust all their precautions."[4]

The legislative power is certainly a double-edged sword at best. Therefore, one way of getting back on the road to freedom is to start focusing a lot more attention on Congress, rather than merely on the president. Most of what we need Congress to do is repeal bad legislation and take power and responsibilities away from the government.

First, all interference into the marketplace by our federal government must cease. This includes bailouts to save corporations that should go bankrupt, inflation of the money supply through the Federal Reserve System, and "stimulus packages" designed to distribute more borrowed or newly printed money from the government. The goal is to allow the free market to liquidate the assets of unprofitable companies and allow those assets to be purchased and reallocated to profitable ventures. While this will cause short term unemployment and an economic downturn, trying to keep those assets and employees permanently allocated to unprofitable companies will only prolong and exacerbate the problem. As opposed to the highly productive American economy with deep savings of 78 years ago, today's America cannot absorb the damage that would be caused by another New Deal.

The Patriot Act, the Military Commissions Act, and the Violent Radicalization and Homegrown Terrorism Prevention Act of 2007 must be repealed. Various Executive Orders issued by President Bush to assume dictatorial powers during a "state of emergency" must be declared without authority and immediately withdrawn.

Cease funding our worldwide military presence, forcing the president to recall our troops from the 130 countries in which they are stationed. This will force a refocus of the mission of the armed services to defend the life, liberty, and property of American citizens and nothing more. During Congressional elections, candidates must be forced to take unambiguous positions on the military budget. They must be put on notice that any vote to perpetuate our military empire will result in their prompt removal from office.

Develop and execute a plan to eliminate (not reform) all government redistribution programs, including corporate welfare, Social Security, Medicare, Medicaid, TANF, farm subsidies, food stamps, and any other programs that forcibly transfer wealth from one individual to another. Care should be taken in this plan to minimize the hardship on those most dependent on the programs during the transition, but that compassion should not be allowed to compromise the ultimate goal. The programs must be completely eliminated and constitutional amendments should be considered to prevent future U.S. legislatures from reinstituting them. Corporate welfare and bailouts can be addressed first. That should be an easy win. Social Security and Medicare should be addressed next. As the drain on savings decreases and subsequent investment and new jobs result, there will be less and less need for the programs for the poor, which should be phased out last.

Repeal the Federal Reserve Act and restore a commodity-backed currency. Develop and execute a plan to move towards a 100% reserve ratio, ending fractional reserve banking. A fiat currency under control by a central bank makes the warfare/welfare state possible. It is also the source of the lion's share of corporate welfare. With the currency stabilized, the economy will naturally reward merit again instead of political connections. As productivity increases, prices will fall and the working class and poor will finally start realizing an improving standard of living again. Abolishing the privilege to inflate the currency will eliminate the wealth transfer from middle class and poor to wealthy, and will diminish the need for the social programs.

Repeal any laws that prohibit actions that do not directly harm another person, such as drug laws, gun laws, and laws that attempt to "prevent crime," rather than prohibit crime. This will end the prison-industrial complex, with its 2.3 million prisoners. It will also cut off the revenue streams of criminal gangs and organizations that currently profit from drugs merely because they are illegal. Without the drug trade, a huge incentive to join gangs will be removed. Most importantly, an enormous drag on the productive efforts of law abiding citizens will be eliminated, restoring the growth and innovation that has been declining in American society for decades.

Repeal any laws that grant government the power to intervene into the marketplace, including "investment" in new technologies or energy sources. There should be no energy policy, education policy, or attempts by government to create jobs or build infrastructure. Government's role in the economy must be limited to preventing force or fraud and enforcing contracts.

Institute a plan to eliminate the income tax. Consider Estonia's solution of a flat tax on all citizens, as opposed to a progressive tax, which is scheduled to decrease every year. Consideration must be made for the huge national debt, or the income tax might be eliminated tomorrow. However, with the savings realized due to the withdrawal of troops from around the world put toward funding the entitlement programs during their phase out period, the lion's share of the income tax can be applied to the principle on the national debt. As that principle decreases, the income tax can decrease, until it is finally reduced to zero. The day the income tax is eliminated is the day liberty is truly restored in America.

That last legislative change should prompt a constitutional one: Repeal the 16th Amendment to ensure an income tax is not easily reinstituted.

We can also restore sovereignty to the states by repealing the 17th Amendment. This will return selection of the senators to the state legislatures, restoring a key check on the power of the federal government. No longer will states take their orders from Washington, as they have for far too long. Washington will again take their orders from the States, which are under even greater control of the people.

In summary, the Constitution of the United States must be strictly enforced upon the federal government, bringing its powers back into the narrowly defined limits in that document, suggested amendments notwithstanding. While far from perfect, the Constitution provided the best defense we had against tyranny while we were still willing to obey it.

Most major party candidates don't even talk about solutions like these. This is no accident. Americans must recognize that the two major parties have completely forgotten or abandoned their duty to the people they supposedly represent. It is time for a massive replacement of our politicians, most importantly in the Congress.

We must elect representatives that will vote these changes into law. Without legal authority, no president can inflict the harm our most recent presidents have inflicted. Without Congressional approval, no president can take us to war. Without Congressional approval, not one dollar of our money can be spent.

There is really very little difference between the two major parties. Neither questions the massive military empire we are maintaining, only what countries we should bomb next. Neither questions the monetary system at all, despite irrefutable proof of its complicity in creating our economic crises. Neither questions the welfare state, morally or practically, even though it violates our most important individual rights and has destroyed the economic stability of our society. There will never be freedom in America again until this political cartel is dismantled. The entrenched ruling parties must be voted out of office with all possible haste.

One might argue there are no viable alternatives to the major party candidates. No so. The various meet-up groups and other organizations that would normally pool their votes to support the "lesser of two evils" can instead select candidates from among themselves. If there was any illusion our entrenched legislators possess some special skill or expertise that makes them more qualified than the average citizen, then surely their performance over the past few years has eliminated that misconception.

While they remain in office, current representatives must be reminded daily of our demands and their responsibility to heed them. Every American must become a political activist. Contrary to old saying "You can't fight city hall," Americans were shown how powerful their voices are during the bailout hearings in 2008. While ultimately unsuccessful in preventing its passage, the thousands of calls and letters to their representatives caused many to vote against the bill, resulting in its initial failure. That was the first time in decades that Americans availed themselves of the right to petition their government. It was only hesitation in the face of subsequent fear mongering that allowed Congress to pass the legislation on the second try. Had average Americans not "blinked," fear of removal from office would have motivated most in Congress to vote it down again.

Politicians ultimately want one thing: to stay in office. We must make it clear that these changes are a condition of them keeping their jobs.

Americans must avail themselves of their right to peacefully assemble and petition the government for redress of grievances. Events have already occurred all over the country to protest the course our government is steering. These events are attended by tens of thousands of Americans. They must be attended by hundreds of thousands. During the 1960's, there were protests on every college campus and in public squares in Washington D.C. and elsewhere, protesting the Viet Nam war. While many of the demands of those activists were honorable, such as civil rights for blacks and an end to an unjust war, that movement also carried with it a message of socialism. We are in need of a similar movement during this young century as well, only this time with a message of liberty. We must not ask for our rights or be grateful for partial victories along the way. We must demand our rights, and let the government see, hear, and feel our power. We are a free people, and must let the government know we are ready to defend that freedom against any and all aggression, including by our government.

At first glance, these suggestions might seem extreme. They are. Extremism in the defense of liberty is a necessity in times like these. As I said at the beginning of this book, rediscovering the principles of liberty forces us to question beliefs and institutions we have always considered unquestionable. Once we take that leap, liberty provides clear, unambiguous answers to our problems. There are no real dilemmas in government, nor any need for compromise of our rights. What is needed is an undistorted view of our place in the world as free individuals. Once we begin to see each other this way again, all of those insoluble dilemmas disappear.

Chapter 15
The Time is at Hand

"If ever time should come, when vain and aspiring men shall possess the highest seats in Government, our country will stand in need of its experienced patriots to prevent its ruin."

– Samuel Adams (1780)[1]

Regardless of their political beliefs, most Americans recognize that our republic is in crisis. While it has been possible in previous decades to put off systemic problems, it is not possible anymore. Our government is bankrupt and cannot make good on the massive promises it has made to its own people any more than it can maintain its military empire around the world. Our system is collapsing and will have to be replaced with another.

It is always easy to blame the incumbent political party and vote in the other. For decades, this has been how Americans have attempted to solve problems that have worsened with each decade. By now, it should be obvious that changing the deck chairs are not going to save the Titanic. While the present leadership is certainly not above criticism, we must look much deeper if we are to regain what has been lost. President Obama won an election with a campaign based upon "change," but he has backed away from even the superficial changes he talked about while campaigning. Worse yet, his changes of substance are exactly what America didn't need.

As free individuals, we must recognize the part we have played ourselves in bringing about the nightmare we are living in. If "vain and aspiring men (and women)" possess the highest seats in government, it is because those are the types of people that acquire power when the people choose to place the government over themselves. When the people look to government to solve their problems, they get public masters instead of public servants.

What is uncertain is what kind of America we will become after the collapse. Will we reawaken liberty, and create a society based upon individual rights and voluntary exchange? Or will we follow the lead of the failed European empires, which chose the debilitating path of socialism?

We have spent a considerable percentage of this short book examining economics and economic freedom. Hopefully, the reader has realized economic freedom is the central freedom. Without owning the product of one's labor, calling an individual free is a little like taking all of Tiger Woods' golf clubs away, except for his putter, and saying he is free to play golf. The right to the product of one's labor is the essence and the means of freedom. Without it, we are little more than slaves, no matter how jealously we guard our rights to free speech, due process, or freedom of religion. When the state owns the individual's labor, it owns the individual.

When the individual is dependent upon government to provide the means of his existence, the government can then place conditions under which those necessities will be provided. Once the state is able to violate rights to achieve its economic goals, it can violate rights to meet any of its goals. Our founding fathers recognized this clearly. They did not tar and feather censors or clergymen; they tarred and feathered tax collectors. The true aim of the tyrant is plunder. This has never changed and will never change.

The great turning points in history have all been a result of economic turmoil. Ancient Rome fell when its currency collapsed, and it could no longer pay for the worldwide military force guarding its empire or the massive welfare programs at home. Germany of the 1920's and 30's brought Adolph Hitler to power amidst a currency collapse, which was as much a result of socialism as it was the ruinous terms of the Treaty of Versailles. The Soviet Union lost its empire and abandoned communism for economic reasons, also accompanied by a collapse of the currency.

America is experiencing all of the same symptoms those failed societies experienced, and for all of the same reasons. Only cultural bias makes us think our situation is different. Economics are at the root of all societal organization. This is something our schools do not stress enough, if at all.

The conditions that exist in the United States today should be alarming to everyone. Never has our government been a greater threat to our freedom. Compared to the "land of opportunity" that we once were, we are increasingly slipping into an authoritarian nightmare.

All that is needed to end any nightmare is to wake up. We are presently going to be forced to make changes. What will those changes be? If we choose wisely, this crisis could be an historic opportunity for a return to freedom and prosperity. If we choose unwisely, the nightmare can get much, much worse.

With the mixed economies and central banking failing all over the world, there is an opportunity to remake our country any way we wish. There is no natural law that says the collapse of one system must give rise to a more oppressive one. It is ultimately the decision of the people that determines which way the pendulum will swing. We must decide freedom is really what we want. That means saying goodbye to the illusion that government can provide for us, and trusting in our own abilities. We must restore respect for individual rights and renew our faith in voluntary exchange. We must reject the use of force as the means to pursue our happiness.

Regardless of what we decide, one positive change that will come out of this crisis will be the end of the American military empire. Economic reality will simply force us to bring our troops home. Military might is rooted in economic might. There is nothing inherently better about American soldiers. Americans are descended from people that came from all over the world. America's military dominance has been the result of its ability to train and equip its soldiers better because of its economic superiority. That economic superiority is gone. The military disparity between the United States and the rest of the world will soon diminish significantly.

What must be avoided is our government treating this as a last chance to plunder what we no longer produce ourselves, while we still have the military capability to do so. Many empires have attempted this in the past, and always with disastrous results.

Our inability to continue to police the world will be good for Americans. With our overseas empire dismantled and our military force limited to defending the United States, the resentment against America will quickly fade. With it will fade the motivation for terrorism. By restoring friendship with all nations, entangling alliances with none, and a policy prohibiting wars of aggression, we can again make America the inspiration of the world. There was a time when the leaders of most Middle Eastern nations admired and sought to emulate the United States. There is no reason that cannot be true again.

At home, once we have recognized that voluntary exchange is the only way for free people to deal with one another, most of our societal problems will begin to solve themselves. With ownership of our labor restored to us, our nation can again be an engine of prosperity, not just for the affluent, but for all Americans. With the gap between rich and poor shrinking once again and the middle class enjoying the explosive growth free markets inevitably foster, far fewer people will face the harsh choices so many face today. For those who still need help, the prosperity we generate will allow us to revive the private charities that once astonished de Tocqueville and inspired the world.

I said at the beginning of this book that all we hold dear about America is in jeopardy. It is. In the not too distant future, the inevitable collapse will occur. With the failure of the old philosophy, a new one will be born. That philosophy will define America in the century ahead, for our children and our grandchildren. This book has attempted to reawaken the spirit of liberty and to persuade Americans to reclaim their natural, inalienable rights. The rest is up to you.

End Notes

Introduction: The American Crisis

1   Paine, Thomas The American Crisis "The Crisis No. 1" December 19, 1776 from Paine Collected Writings edited by Eric Foner Literary Classics of the United States, Inc. New York, NY 1955 pg. 91

Chapter 1: What is Freedom?

1   Bastiat, Frederic The Law 1850 from The Bastiat Collection 2 Volumes Vol. 1 Ludwig Von Mises Institute Auburn, AL 2007 pg. 79

2   Madison,   James   Federalist   #10
    http://www.foundingfathers.info/federalistpapers/fedi.htm
    http://www.foundingfathers.info/federalistpapers/fed10.htm

3   Madison, James Letter to James Monroe October 5th, 1786 James Madison Center, The http://www.jmu.edu/madison/center/home.htm Phillip Bigler, Director,   James   Madison   University   Harrisonburg,   VA http://www.jmu.edu/madison/center/main_pages/madison_archives/quotes/supr emacy.htm

4   Jefferson, Thomas To Dupont de Nemours from Jefferson Writings edited by Merrill D. Peterson New York, NY: Literary Classics of the United States, 1984 pg. 1387

5   Declaration of Independence, United States 1776 National Archives and Records (website) http://www.archives.gov/exhibits/charters/declaration_transcript.html

6   John Locke Second Treatise on Civil Government from Two Treatises of Government C. and J. Rivington, 1824 (Harvard University Library Copy) pg. 132

7   Declaration of Independence, United States 1776 National Archives...

8   Locke Second Treatise pgs. 131-32

9   Locke Second Treatise pg. 133

10   Adams, John A Dissertation on the Canon and Feudal Law 1765 Ashland Center for   Public   Affairs   (website)   Ashland   University http://www.ashbrook.org/library/18/adams/canonlaw.html

Chapter 2: Property Rights

1   Adams, Samuel The Rights of the Colonists (1772) The Report of the Committee of Correspondence to the Boston Town Meeting, Nov. 20, 1772 from Old South Leaflets no. 173 edited by Edwin Doak Mead Old South Meeting House 1903 pgs. 417-428.

2   Locke Second Treatise pgs. 146-47

Chapter 3: The Role of Government

1   Jefferson, Thomas Letter to Francis Walker Gilmer June 7, 1816 from The Works of Thomas Jefferson edited by Paul Leicester Ford G.P. Putnam's Sons New York and London The Knickerbocker Press 1905 pg. 533-34

2   Locke Second Treatise pg.204

3   Locke Second Treatise pg. 204

4   Declaration of Independence National Archives...

5   Locke Second Treatise pg. 210

6   Locke Second Treatise pg.213

7   Paine, Thomas The Rights of Man Part the Second Ch. IV from Paine Collected Writings edited by Eric Foner Literary Classics of the United States, Inc. New York, NY 1955

8   Paine, Thomas The Rights of Man Part the Second Ch. IV from Paine Collected Writings edited by Eric Foner Literary Classics of the United States, Inc. New York, NY 1955

9   Washington, George (Attributed). Scholars have correctly pointed out that this quote cannot be found in Washington's Farewell Address of 1796, or in any other written record of Washington's writings or speeches. It may very well be apocryphal, but certainly sums up the founders' suspicion of government.

10. Jefferson, Thomas Letter to Joseph Milligan April 6, 1816 (regarding Destutt de Tracy's Treatise on Political Economy) from The Writings of Thomas Jefferson, Vol. 14 edited by Albert Ellery Bergh and Andrew A. Lipscomb The Thomas Jefferson Memorial Association 1904 pg. 466

11 Jefferson, Thomas 2nd Inaugural Address (1805) from Jefferson Writings edited by Merrill D. Peterson Literary Classics of the United States, New York, NY 1984 pg. 522

12 It also indicates quite clearly that Jefferson did not wish to destroy the rights of inheritance. Jefferson successfully had the laws of primogeniture repealed in Virginia, which actually enhanced property rights. Primogeniture forced the bequeather to leave his property solely to the first-born son, without the option to dispose of it as he wished. Repealing primogeniture allowed the bequeather to leave his property to anyone he wished, therefore giving him more property rights, not less. Repealing primogeniture gave no authority for the state to make any claims upon, nor interfere with the transfer of property from the bequeather to the bequeathed.

13 Bastiat The Law, Bastiat Collection pg. 51

14 Bastiat The Law, Bastiat Collection pg. 52

15 Bastiat The Law, Bastiat Collection pg. 62

16 Corporate welfare is usually accomplished through the insidious practice of inflation, where the corporations receive loans from the Federal Reserve based upon new money created out of thin air. While the corporations may eventually pay the loans back, the money creation dilutes the value each U.S. dollar, thus

forcing an "invisible tax" upon the rest of society. While this practice is somewhat more opaque and indirect, it is no less wealth redistribution and a violation of property rights. We will explore the details more in a later chapter.

17 Bastiat The Law, Bastiat Collection pg. 61

18 BBC News Thursday, 27 September, 2001 "Switzerland and the Gun" http://news.bbc.co.uk/2/hi/europe/1566715.stm

19 Webster, Noah An Examination of the Leading Principles of the Federal Constitution (Philadelphia 1787). from The Essential Federalist and Anti-Federalist Papers edited by David Wootton Hackett Publishing Company Indianapolis, IN 2003 Pg. 132

20 Bastiat The Law, Bastiat Collection pg. 62

21 Paul, Ron The Revolution: A Manifesto Grand Central Publishing New York, NY (2008) pg. x

Chapter 4: The State of War

1   Madison, James Political Observations 1795 from Letters and Other Writings of James Madison J.P. Lippincott & Co. Philadelphia, PA 1865 pg. 492

2   U.S. Constitution Article I Section 8 National Archives... http://www.archives.gov/exhibits/charters/constitution_transcript.html

3   Locke Second Treatise pgs. 140-41

4   Locke Second Treatise pgs. 140

5   The philosophies of Hobbes and Rousseau were fundamentally quite different and ultimately irreconcilable with Locke's. Rousseau believed that people had to give up their individual rights to enter into the "social contract" of civil society, and that once in society one's rights were determined by the group, including property rights. Hobbes believed that man existed in a perpetual state of war in nature, and that a strong central government was required to prevent civil war once man entered the social contract. Neither philosophy ultimately allowed for the individual liberty of Locke that inspired the American Revolution. However, despite these fundamental differences, there is much common ground between

them when addressing the state of war, which is the great destroyer of liberty, no matter whose definition is used.

6   Hobbes, Thomas, The Leviathan Chapter XIII (1651) Forgotten Books 2008 http://forgottenbooks.org pg. 86

7   Rousseau, Jean-Jacques WHAT IS THE ORIGIN OF INEQUALITY AMONG MEN, AND IS IT AUTHORISED BY NATURAL LAW? Part II from The Social Contract & Discourses by Jean Jacques Rousseau E.P. Dutton New York, NY 1913 pg. 222

8   That the definition of the state of war applies not only to individuals, but to states as well is made clear by Locke in later chapters.

9
        http://www.sagehistory.net/jeffersonjackson/documents/MadisonWarMessage.htm

10 Twelfth   Congress   Sess.   1,   Ch.   102
    http://www.lawandfreedom.com/site/historical/GBritain1812.pdf

11 http://www.pbs.org/weta/thewest/resources/archives/two/mexdec.htm

12 Twenty-Ninth   Congress   Sess.   I   Ch.   16
    http://www.lawandfreedom.com/site/historical/Mexico1846.pdf

13 http://www.spanamwar.com/McKinleywardec.htm

14 Fifty-fifth   Congress   Sess.   II.   Ch.   189
    http://www.lawandfreedom.com/site/historical/Spain1898.pdf

15 http://historymatters.gmu.edu/d/4943/

16 Sixty-Fifth   Congress   Ch.   1
    http://www.lawandfreedom.com/site/historical/Germany1917.pdf

17 http://www.americanrhetoric.com/speeches/fdrpearlharbor.htm

18 Seventy-seventh   Congress   Sess.   1   Ch.   561
    http://www.lawandfreedom.com/site/historical/Japan1941.pdf

19 Locke Second Treatise pg. 142

20 Washington, George Farewell Address, September 19, 1796 from Peck, William T. Washington's Farewell Address and Webster's Bunker Hill Orations The MacMillan Company New York, NY 1919 pg. 25

21 Jefferson, Thomas First Inaugural Address March 4, 1801 from Jefferson Writings pg. 494

22 There have been interesting and very reasonable arguments made that even WWI and WWII were not necessary for the United States. While this is generally considered the equivalent in political/historical discourse as "sacrilege," it is an argument that is not easily dismissed. In any case, it is clear that at least since WWII, every war or other military action that the U.S. has been involved in has been unnecessary and therefore a violation of the rights of its citizens.

Chapter 5: The Economics of Liberty

1   Smith, Adam An Inquiry into the Wealth of Nations from An Inquiry into the Wealth of Nations: Selections edited by Laurance Winant Dickey Hackett Publishing Indianapolis, IN 1993 pg. 165

2   http://www.merriam-webster.com/dictionary/economics

3   The quote from Wealth of Nations in the prologue of this chapter demonstrates that the Non-aggression principle is inseparable from capitalism. Smith is unable to talk about one without inherently talking about the other.

4   Smith Wealth of Nations Selections pg. 165

5   http://www.merriam-webster.com/dictionary/capitalism

6   Smith Wealth of Nations Selections pg. 130

7   Bernstein, Andrew The Capitalist Manifesto: The Historic, Economic and Philosophic Case for Laissez Faire University Press of America Lanham, MD 2005 pgs. 58-59.

8   Real wages refers to the purchasing power of the wages earned, rather than their nominal value. For example, if an employee's wages remain the same, but all prices decrease by 50%, then his "real wages" have doubled, because he can buy twice as much with the same amount of money. This was one reason for the

rapid increase in quality of life for the working class during the industrial revolution.

9   Bernstein Capitalist Manifesto pgs. 128-29.

10   Hayek, Friedrich The Road to Serfdom (1944) Routledge 270 Madison Avenue, New York, NY 10016 pgs. 51-52

11   While the earliest thinkers of this school came from Austria, the "Austrian school" today includes economists from many different countries, including the United States.

12   This is admittedly an oversimplification, which notably excludes the Monetarists and other schools.   The other schools can be more closely associated with Keynesianism than with the Austrian school, if for no other reason than they argue for government control of the money supply and stabilization of prices, rather than market forces determining each. It should not be forgotten, though, that many Monetarists, such as Milton Friedman, argued vehemently for free market capitalism, with the exception of government manipulation of the money supply and interest rates, which is nevertheless a fatal flaw in their argument for "free markets." It can also be argued that in recent decades, government has moved away from a Keynesian philosophy to a more Monetarist one, although it is apparent that the current crisis is already prompting government to shift back towards Keynesianism.

13   This does not assume the absence of government, despite the repeated attempts by adversaries of liberty to raise this straw man. It assumes government limited to its proper and very necessary role – to protect the life, liberty, and property of individuals against aggression by other individuals or groups.

14   Without delving too far into the theoretical differences between Smith and the Austrians, the reader may look into the subjectivist approach to economics, which has its roots in Carl Menger's Principles of Economics (1871). Rather than refute Smith's arguments for laissez faire, subjectivism actually lends more support for laissez faire than Smith's labor theory of value was able to substantiate.

15   The conventional wisdom that WWII pulled America out of the Great Depression

is another misconception that proceeds from the Keynesian assumptions.

16   Schiff, Peter (with John Downes) Crash Proof: How to Profit from the Coming Economic Collapse John Wiley & Sons, Inc. Hoboken, NJ 2007

17   It should be noted that neither Hoover nor the Congress has any statutory authority to control the Federal Reserve. In fact, the Federal Reserve Act actually prohibits government from directing the actions of this private banking cartel. Hoover's failure was his reaction to the crash, not any role he had in creating the boom.

18   One cannot help recalling George Bush's paradoxical statement that he is a proponent of the free market, but that the "market is not functioning properly." Only a politician could be capable of such nonsense.

19   Rothbard, Murray America's Great Depression (1963) from the Fifth Edition ©2000 by The Ludwig Von Mises Institute Auburn Alabama pgs. 285-86

20   It is noteworthy that this bill was actually signed by President Clinton, not the supposedly laissez faire President Bush. It was this bill that enabled the creation of the modern derivative market that is suspected of totaling tens of trillions of dollars.

21   This was also a key policy of Clinton's, who appointed Franklin D. Raines (FDR II?) to his post at Fannie Mae and did everything he could to encourage the expansion of Fannie Mae and Freddie Mac, including the massive increase in risk that the GSE's undertook. While Clinton himself was only one part of the government at the time, and the author believes that presidents ultimately get too much blame and too much credit for just about everything, if one is looking for a president to blame for the housing bubble, it is rightly Clinton instead of Bush.

Chapter 6: The Money Monopoly

1   Jefferson, Thomas Letter to Abbe Salimankis (1810) from Writings of Thomas Jefferson Bergh and Lipscomb pg. 379-380

2   Federal Reserve Bank of Minneapolis Official Website http://www.minneapolisfed.org/community_education/teacher/calc/hist1800.cfm

3   Bank failures are, of course, not the only causes of deflation. In theory, deflation also occurs when loans are paid back at a faster rate than new money is created. However, this has been the exception rather than the rule over the past century. Aggregated together, the century has been one of massive inflation.

4   Huerta De Soto, Jesus Money, Banking, and Economic Cycles (English Edition) Ludwig Von Mises Institute Auburn, Alabama 2006 pg. 713

5   Huerta de Soto, Money, Bank Credit... pgs. 317-346.

6   Huerta de Soto Money, Bank Credit... pgs. 347-84

7   This is a very general and simplified explanation of malinvestment and economic bubbles. For a more thorough explanation, the reader is encouraged to read Jose Huerta de Soto's Money, Bank Credit, and Economic Cycles, especially Chapters 5 & 6 on this particular subject.

8   Huerta De Soto, Money, Bank Credit...pgs. 736-812

Chapter 7: The Non-Rights

1   Adams, John A Defense of the Constitutions of Government of the United States of America (1787) from The Works of John Adams Charles C. Little and James Brown Boston, MA 1851 pg. 9

2   Bernstein The Capitalist Manifesto, pg. 241.

Chapter 8: The Slavery Tax

1   Charles de Secondat, Baron de Montesquieu The Spirit of Laws Book XIII Sec. 14 trans. by Thomas Nugent The Colonial Press New York 1900 pg. 215

2   Locke Second Treatise pgs. 204-5

3   Locke Second Treatise pgs. 205

4   Madison, James from The Debates and Proceedings in the Congress of the United States edited by Joseph Gales Gales and Seaton Washington 1834 pg. 102

5   Jefferson, Thomas 2nd Inaugural Address March 4, 1805 from Jefferson Writings

pg. 518

6   Resolutions of Congress on Lord North's Conciliatory Proposal July 31, 1775 from Jefferson Writings pg. 332

7   The   Tax   Foundation   Washington,   D.C. http://www.taxfoundation.org/research/show/1962.html

Chapter 9: The Socialism Bubble

1   Jefferson, Thomas Letter to Edward Bancroft, January 26, 1788 from Writings of Thomas Jefferson Bergh and Lipscomb pg. 41

2   The lack of understanding of "real wages" was certainly not the social reformers only misconception, but it was representative of others.   Even today, our government still warns us against the horrors of "deflation," despite clear evidence that deflation benefits the majority of society, most notably responsible savers.

3   It is conceivable that the Federal Reserve could inflate the currency so much that the stock market remains at $11,000. However, if at some point $11,000 only buys 10 loaves of bread, it would still represent the same devaluation as a crash.

Chapter 10: The War On . . .

1   Pennsylvania Assembly: Reply to the Governor, Tue, Nov 11, 1755. There is some controversy over whether Franklin was actually the source of this quote, which appeared in the anonymously published "An Historical Review of the Constitution and Government of Pennsylvania" in 1759.   While most attribute the Historical Review to Franklin, he actually denied it in a letter to David Hume (September 27, 1760).   Whatever its original source, the wisdom of the statement is self-evident.

2   This is a reality of war that the United States did not have to face in the 20th century, mainly due to its geographic isolation from the other major powers of the industrialized world.

3   U.S.   Constitution,   Fifth   Amendment   National   Archives... http://www.archives.gov/exhibits/charters/bill_of_rights_transcript.html

4   U.S.   Department   of   Justice   Bureau   of   Justice   Statistics   (website)

http://www.ojp.usdoj.gov/bjs/fed.htm#Adjudication

5   In 2008, some successful challenges to these guidelines have resulted in the compulsory requirement of judges to adhere to the guidelines being lifted. However, they are so firmly established that few judges vary far from them.

6   United States Sentencing Commission, Guidelines Manual, §3E1.1 (Nov. 2006) http://www.ussc.gov/2006guid/gl2006.pdf

7   Bureau of Justice Statistics http://www.ojp.usdoj.gov/bjs/prisons.htm

8   The REX 84 Alpha Explan was acknowledged by Ollie North during the Iran-Contra hearings, but has received little attention recently in the mainstream media.

9   Cavallaro, Gina Army Times "Brigade Homeland Tours Start Oct. 1" Sept. 30, 2008 http://www.armytimes.com/news/2008/09/army_homeland_090708w/

10   Video here: http://www.youtube.com/watch?v=Df2p6867_pw

Chapter 11: The Media Monolith

1   Jefferson, Thomas Letter to G.K. van Hogendrop October 13, 1785 Jefferson Writings Peterson pg. 835

2   Dowell, William "Saddam Turns His Back on Greenbacks" Time November 13, 2000 http://www.time.com/time/magazine/article/0,9171,998512,00.html

3   Mortished, Carl "Iran turns from dollar to euro in oil sales" The London Times December 22, 2006 (references announcement by Iran in 2004) http://business.timesonline.co.uk/tol/business/economics/article1263954.ece

4   "Venezuela Mulls euro oil switch" BBC News December 22, 2006

5   http://en.wikipedia.org/wiki/Communications_Act_of_1934

Chapter 12: False Prophets of Freedom

1   Attributed to Byles by James R. Gilmore, based upon he recollection of Rev. Dr. Nathaniel Emmons from New England Magazine New Series Vol. 16, Old Series Vol. 22 Warren F. Kellogg, Publisher Boston, MA 1897 pg. 735

2   Bastiat, Frederic The Law (1850) (words in parentheses added) The Bastiat Collection pg. 61

3   Madison,   James   Federalist   #10
    http://www.foundingfathers.info/federalistpapers/fed10.htm

4   Hayek, Road to Serfdom pg. 91

Chapter 13: Extremism in the Defense of Liberty

1   Henry, Patrick at Virginia Convention March 23, 1775 from Brewer, David The World's Best Orations from the Earliest Period to the Present Time Vol. 7 Ferd P.Kaiser 1901 pg. 2477

2   Hall, Joseph Christian Moderation from Wynter, Philip D.D. The Works of the Right Reverend Joseph Hall, D.D. Oxford at the University Press 1863 pg. 388

Chapter 14: The Road to Freedom

1   Paine, Thomas Common Sense (1776) from Paine Writings pg. 52

2   LaRosa,   Benedict   D.   Democracy   or   Republic,   Which   Is   It?
    http://www.devvy.com/pdf/larosa/larosa_democracy_or_republic.pdf pg. 11

3   Madison, James to Thomas Jefferson October 17, 1788 from The Writings of James Madison Vol. 5 1787-1790 edited by Gaillard Hunt G.P. Putnam's Sons Knickerbocker Press New York, NY 1904 pg. 272

4   Madison,   James   Federalist   No.   48   (1787)
    http://www.foundingfathers.info/federalistpapers/fedindex.htm

Chapter 15: The Time is at Hand

1   Adams, Samuel Letter to James Warren October 24, 1780 from The Writings of Samuel Adams edited by Harry Alonzo Cushing G.P. Putnam's Sons Knickerbocker Press New York, NY 1908 pg. 213

Bibliography

Adams, John The Works of John Adams Second President of the United States Charles C. Little and James Brown Boston, MA 1851

Adams, Samuel The Writings of Samuel Adams edited by Harry Alonzo Cushing G.P. Putnam's Sons Knickerbocker Press New York, NY 1908

Ashbrook Center for Public Affairs (website) http://www.ashbrook.org, Ashland University, Ashland Ohio

Bastiat, Frederic The Bastiat Collection 2 Volumes Vol. 1 Ludwig Von Mises Institute Auburn, AL 2007

Bernstein, Andrew The Capitalist Manifesto: The Historic, Economic, and Philosophic Case for Laissez Faire. Lanham, MD: University Press of America, 2005

Brewer, David The World's Best Orations from the Earliest Period to the Present Time Vol. 7 Ferd P.Kaiser 1901

Destutt de Tracy, Comte Antoine Louis Claude A Treatise of Political Economy trans. Thomas Jefferson (1817) Augustus M. Kelley Publishers New York, NY 1970

Federal Reserve Bank of Minneapolis (website) http://www.minneapolisfed.org

Ford, Paul Leicester The Works of Thomas Jefferson G.P. Putnam's Sons New York and London The Knickerbocker Press 1905

Founding Fathers (website) www.foundingfathers.info Chris Witten, Webmaster

Gales, Joseph The Debates and Proceedings in the Congress of the United States

Gales and Seaton Washington 1834

Hobbes, Thomas Leviathan (1651) Forgotten Books 2008 http://forgottenbooks.org

Huerta De Soto, Jesus Money, Banking, and Economic Cycles (English Edition) Ludwig Von Mises Institute Auburn, Alabama 2006

Hunt, Gaillard The Writings of James Madison Vol. 5 1787-1790 G.P. Putnam's Sons Knickerbocker Press New York, NY 1904

James Madison Center, The http://www.jmu.edu/madison/center/home.htm Phillip Bigler, Director, James Madison University Harrisonburg, VA

Jefferson, Thomas Jefferson Writings edited by Merrill D. Peterson, Literary Classics of the United States, New York, NY 1984

Jefferson, Thomas The Works of Thomas Jefferson edited by Paul Leicester Ford G.P. Putnam's Sons New York and London The Knickerbocker Press 1905

Jefferson, Thomas The Writings of Thomas Jefferson, Bergh, Albert Ellery and Lipscomb, Andrew A. (editors) The Thomas Jefferson Memorial Association 1904

Library of Congress, American Memory Collection (website) http://memory.loc.gov/ammem/index.html

Locke, John Two Treatises of Government C. and J. Rivington, 1824 (Harvard University Library Copy)

Madison, James Letters and other Writings of James Madison J.P. Lippincott & Co. Philadelphia, PA 1865

Mead, Edwin Doak Old South Leaflets, Twenty-first Series Old South Meeting House, Boston, MA 1903

Montesquieu, Charles de Secondat, Baron de The Spirit of the Laws (1748) trans. By Thomas Nugent The Colonial Press New York 1900

National Archives and Records Administration (website) http://www.archives.gov/

New England Magazine New Series Vol. 16, Old Series Vol. 22 Warren F. Kellogg, Publisher Boston, MA 1897

Paine, Thomas Paine Collected Writings edited by Eric Foner Literary Classics of the United States, Inc. New York, NY 1955

Paul, Ron The Revolution: A Manifesto Grand Central Publishing New York, NY 2008

Peck, William T. Washington's Farewell Address and Webster's Bunker Hill Orations The MacMillan Company New York, NY 1919

Rothbard, Murray America's Great Depression Fifth Edition Ludwig Von Mises Institute Auburn, AL 2000

Rousseau, Jean Jacques The Social Contract & Discourses by Jean Jacques Rousseau E.P. Dutton New York, NY 1913

Schiff, Peter (with John Downes) Crash Proof: How to Profit from the Coming Economic Collapse John Wiley & Sons, Inc. Hoboken, NJ 2007

Smith, Adam An Inquiry into the Wealth of Nations: Selections edited by Laurance Winant Dickey Hackett Publishing Indianapolis, IN 1993

U.S. Department of Justice Bureau of Justice Statistics (website) http://www.ojp.usdoj.gov/bjs

United States Sentencing Commission, Guidelines Manual, §3E1.1 (Nov. 2006)

Wootton, David (editor) The Essential Federalist and Anti-Federalist Papers Hackett Publishing Company Indianapolis, IN 2003

Wynter, Philip D.D. The Works of the Right Reverend Joseph Hall, D.D. Oxford at the University Press 1863

Made in the USA
Lexington, KY
27 November 2016